ANN BASSETT

Colorado's Cattle Queen

Linda Wommack

Caxton Press

Dedicated to the
memory of
Anna M. Bassett
1878 - 1956

© 2018 by Linda Wommack

First Edition

LCCN# 2017058814
CIP Information available at Loc.gov

Library of Congress Cataloging-in-Publication Data

Names: Wommack, Linda, 1958- author.

Title: Ann Bassett : Colorado's cattle queen / by Linda Wommack.
Other titles: Colorado's cattle queen

Description: Caldwell, Idaho : Caxton Press, [2017] | Includes
   bibliographical references and index.

Identifiers: LCCN 2017058814 (print) | LCCN 2018007067
(ebook) | ISBN 9780870046209 | ISBN 9780870046193 (alk. paper)

Subjects: LCSH: Bassett, Ann, 1878-1956 | Women ranchers--Colorado
--Biography. | Ranch life--Colorado--History--19th century. | Outlaws--
Colorado--Biography. | Frontier and pioneer life--Colorado. | Ranchers
--Colorado--Biography. | Women--Colorado--Biography. | Browns Park
--Biography.

Classification: LCC F781 (ebook) | LCC F781 .W86 2017 (print) | DDC
   978.8/02092 [B] --dc23

LC record available at https://lccn.loc.gov/2017058814

Cover and book design by Jocelyn Robertson

Printed in the United States of America
CAXTON PRESS
Caldwell, Idaho
199733

TABLE OF CONTENTS

⇒ FOREWORD ⇐

◇◇◇◇◇◇◇

"Seldom any splendid story is all true," observed Samuel Johnson. A couple hundred years later, Janet Malcom added that "under Gresham's law of biography, good stories drive out true stories."

Brown's Park pioneer Ann Bassett is a case in point. The biographer faces a confusing tangle of the true, not so true, and fantastic. Colliding anecdotes, cherished family stories at war with documentary evidence. The passage of time. Untangling the confusion takes skill and diligence.

Linda Wommack has both. A veteran *Wild West* and *True West* writer, she knows Colorado history, and just as importantly knows her way around the most obscure local archives. That knowledge enabled her to turn up long-neglected documents and settle Bassett controversies.

If no one was better prepared to thrive in 19th and early-20th century Brown's Park than Ann Bassett, no one is better prepared to write her biography than Linda Wommack.

– Daniel Buck & Anne Meadows

⇒ ACKNOWLEDGMENTS ⇐

◇◇◇◇◇◇◇◇◇◇◇◇

I am indebted to many writers who included Anna M. Bassett in their various works regarding the history of Brown's Park. Among these writers is the esteemed regional historian John Rolfe Burroughs' *Where the Old West Stayed Young*, Diana Allen Kouris' *The Romantic and Notorious History of Brown's Park*, and Grace McClure's *The Bassett Women*.

Ann Bassett Willis wrote of her life experiences in a four-part series published in the Colorado Historical Society's *Colorado Magazine*. The series, titled, "Queen Ann of Brown's Park," which ran in Volume XXIX January 1952, Volume XXIX April 1952, Volume XXIX October 1952, Volume XXX January 1953. My thanks goes to the diligent work of friend, Coi E. Drummond-Gerhig, Digital Image Collection Administrator for the Denver Public Library, who provided the complete series written by Ann.

Throughout my own research I began to dispel myths and flush out the truth. Initially, this was a daunting task, as Ann herself was known to embellish and exaggerate. Anna Marie Bassett has largely been an enigma in American outlaw history. Conversely, she is a legend in Colorado history. But she did not invent events.

As my research intensified, I began uncovering supporting evidence to many of Ann's accounts. The best source of documents, court records, unpublished manuscripts, handwritten letters and historic photographs for this work was the extraordinary Museum of Northwest Colorado in Craig, Colorado. Many hours were spent with the Director of the museum, Dan Davidson who patiently answered my questions and pointed me in the right direction. Many more hours were spent with Assistant Director, Jan Gerber, as we went through filing cabinets, boxes, and computer files gathering the needed information. What a pleasure it was when I asked for something, almost without exception, Gerber would reply, "Yes, we have that." I will never forget my visits to the Museum of Northwest Colorado. Their efforts greatly enhanced this work.

In the summer of 2014, I had the pleasure to finally meet Valentine Hoy IV. Hoy not only graciously answered my many questions about his pioneering family of Brown's Park, he also provided documents as well as a digital copy of his great-great uncle's unpublished memoir. In May 1920, James "Jessie" Shade Hoy completed his manuscript of the history of Brown's Park. He wrote a letter to Horace Bennett in Denver, dated August 29, 1924, in which he asked for assistance in finding a publisher for his book. Evidently Bennett was unable or unwilling to help Hoy. A second letter seeking assistance was sent to Governor William E. Sweet, dated September 22, 1924. Hoy was never able to get his book published. Fortunately, two copies of the original manuscript titled, "History of Brown's Hole" survive. One copy can be found in the archives of the Colorado History Center. The other is in the possession of Valentine Hoy, IV.

Over the years of research, I reached out to fellow researchers and friends. Anne Meadows, author of *Digging Up Butch Cassidy*, and her husband Dan Buck were always willing to help. Donna Ernst, author of *Sundance, My Uncle*, and *The Sundance Kid*, was instrumental in providing me with a copy of the only known signature of the elusive Ethel "Etta" Place. This was vital in gathering the many pieces of historical evidence proving that Etta Place and Ann Bassett were not the same person, a ridiculous assumption writers have carried on for years.

Throughout outlaw history circles, much has been written regarding the "Outlaw Thanksgiving." As is so often the case, writers repeat what others have written without researching or verifying sources. In most accounts of the "Outlaw Thanksgiving," the date given as 1895 is attributed to Ann Bassett. Because Ann says Butch Cassidy was in attendance, writers have accused Ann of fabricating the event, because Cassidy was in prison in 1895. However, in all of Ann's writings, published and unpublished, she never mentioned the year of the event. True to her female nature,

Ann focused more on what she wore and how fine she looked. In 1953, Ann's dear friend, Esther Anderson Campbell, wrote a program reenacting the event, based on Ann's account. This is the first known mention of the 1895 date as Campbell titled the program "Thanksgiving 1895." One the many writers repeating the 1895 date was William Tennent, an employee of the Bureau of Land Management in Vernal, Utah. In his 1981 master's thesis, Tennent attributed the 1895 date to a letter written by Ann to Esther Campbell which was supposedly in the archives of the BLM. Thanks to the fine research of Kathie Davies at the BLM Vernal office, it was concluded that no such letter exists. Further inquiries led me to the library and museum at Vernal. Sam Passee was a great research asset, as was LeeAnn Denzer at the Uintah County Heritage Museum. Michelle Fuller at the Uintah County Library went above and beyond the call, providing me with access to their Esther Campbell collection. Again, no such letter from Ann Bassett using the 1895 date. However, there are several letters where Ann chastises Esther for misrepresenting history during the time the two women were collaborating on a book of Brown's Park history. In the archives of the Uintah County Library, Michelle opened my eyes to a copy of Ann Bassett's little known diary, something no writer or researcher has ever mentioned. Michelle was also instrumental in providing me with several photographs, some never before published.

To round out the historic photographs provided by the Uintah County Library and the Museum of Northwest Colorado, I relied on the fabulous work of friend, Coi E. Drummond-Gerhig, Digital Image Collection Administrator for the Denver Public Library.

Special thanks go to those who believed in this project and gave freely of their time and advice. First on that list is my husband Frank, who tolerated the many late nights of research and writing, and helped to work out the research obstacles.

Throughout the research and writing process, I relied on my dear friend, Connie Clayton. Her cogent comments and careful editing strengthened this work immensely. I owe her my heartfelt thanks. Fellow researcher, writer, and my friend, Dan Buck, became my support line when I ran into a few road blocks. Through his advice and encouragement, he kept me from straying too far from my goal.

Finally my sincere thanks to Anna Marie Bassett. She lived an extraordinary life and did what she had to do to protect her family and land. Against all odds, she succeeded. I am proud to bring her life story to all.

– Linda Wommack, August 12, 2016

⇒ INTRODUCTION ⇐

◇◇◇◇◇◇◇◇◇◇

Legend, lore, mystery, romance and even murder, these
are only a few of the many controversies surrounding the life of
"Queen Ann," the legend of Brown's Park. Ann Bassett became
one of the most noted frontier women in Colorado, and gained a
reputation as one of the toughest in the West.

What a woman Ann must have been! She was small in
stature with dark hair and pretty features, and possessed a high-
spirited personality. At a very early age she could ride a horse,
handle a gun, and curse as well as any man on the Bassett family
ranch.

Ann's associations with known outlaws such as Butch
Cassidy and Elza Lay have spawned countless tales of romance,
all untrue. What is true are the accounts of murderous outlaws
in the region. Ann, as well as her sister Josephine, and even J. S.
Hoy, wrote extensive accounts. Their various writings include the
hanging of John Jack "Judge" Bennett from the gate post of the
Bassett ranch. Hoy also provides a personal account of the murder
of his brother Valentine S. Hoy during the manhunt for outlaws
Harry Tracy and David Lant.

In an era when women were expected to keep house
and raise children, Ann lived her life as she pleased, and when
necessary, as she had to. The skills Ann learned as a child would
serve her well when she later waged a one woman vendetta against
her nemesis, Ora Haley, one of the many cattle barons with designs
on taking over as much prime grazing land as possible, by any
means possible.

When Haley and other owners of the larger cattle
companies secretly hired the known killer, Tom Horn, to clean
out the "rustlers" in Brown's Park, it soon became very personal

to Ann. In July 1900, Ann's fiancé, Madison Matthew Rash was murdered at his cabin by none other than Tom Horn.

Ann set out to not only avenge the murder of Rash, but to destroy Ora Haley, who secretly approved the hiring of Horn, and stop his takeover of Brown's Park. By her own account, Ann used extreme measures to reach her goal.

This account of the life of Anna M. Bassett is particularly enhanced by Ann's own words. In her later years Ann put pen to paper, providing her own account of the many now historical events of her beloved Brown's Park. Through her prism, we learn of the rugged pioneers building a life in an isolated corner of Northwestern Colorado, and the many trials and tribulations they faced and overcame.

Through the writings of both friends and enemies of Ann's we also learn of friendships and personal animosities. Leath Avvon Chew, Esther Anderson Campbell, and Rosalie Miles DeJournette wrote warmly of their lifelong friendship with Ann. Hiram "Hi" Bernard, Ann's first husband seemed to have mixed feelings regarding his ex-wife, although he did get into a fist fight defending her honor with another of Ann's enemies, cattle baron J. S. Hoy.

We also learn, through Bernard's reminisces with Francis "Frank" Willis, that Bernard knew that Tom Horn was hired by his boss, Ora Haley, to "clean up" Brown's Park, a fact he denied during much of his lifetime.

This is the story of the Cattle Queen, Anna M. Bassett, who lived through mystery, murder, vendetta, and vengeance.

ANN BASSETT

Colorado's
Cattle Queen

Author's Note:
    Unless otherwise noted within brackets, the quotes
contained within the book include all the spelling, typographical,
grammatical, and syntactical errors as found in their original
published form.

Brown's Park

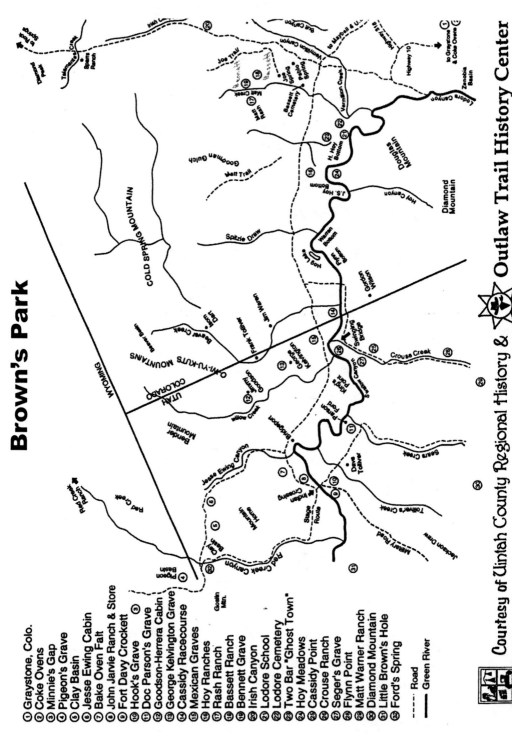

① Graystone, Colo.
② Coke Ovens
③ Minnie's Gap
④ Pigeon's Grave
⑤ Clay Basin
⑥ Jesse Ewing Cabin
⑦ Bake Oven Falt
⑧ John Jarvie Ranch & Store
⑨ Fort Davy Crockett
⑩ Hook's Grave
⑪ Doc Parson's Grave
⑫ Goodson-Herrera Cabin
⑬ George Kelvington Grave
⑭ Cassidy Racecourse
⑮ Mexican Graves
⑯ Hoy Ranches
⑰ Rash Ranch
⑱ Bassett Ranch
⑲ Bennett Grave
⑳ Irish Canyon
㉑ Lodore School
㉒ Lodore Cemetery
㉓ Two Bar "Ghost Town"
㉔ Hoy Meadows
㉕ Cassidy Point
㉖ Crouse Ranch
㉗ Seger's Grave
㉘ Flynn Point
㉙ Matt Warner Ranch
㉚ Diamond Mountain
㉛ Little Brown's Hole
㉜ Ford's Spring

----- Road
—— Green River

Courtesy of Uintah County Regional History & ✳ Outlaw Trail History Center

10

BROWN'S HOLE

The area first known as Brown's Hole is a fertile valley, stretching through miles of sagebrush to the north, where a rocky mountain wonderland runs north by northwest to the borders of Wyoming and Utah. The Green River winds through the valley with Vermilion Creek flowing west of the Bassett ranch. From there, the river flows south through the Gates of Lodore, a narrow rock canyon with mountain ranges on both the west and east. With few entrances in and out of the area, bordering on both the Utah and Wyoming state lines, the area was known as Colorado's legendary "Outlaw Hideout."

It was a brutal area in the northwestern corner of Colorado with the intense heat of long summer days, the sun beating down on the desolate area of a no man's land, and even worse in winter with strong winds often creating blizzard conditions. Only the strongest of pioneers could survive. In this rugged corner of Colorado, Ann Bassett not only survived, but lived to tell the tale. She would become a female enigma.

Ann later described her beloved home, a place she said, "Was the only thing I selfishly loved," as:

> From a country to the northward and far on towards the sunset, flows the mighty Green River. In northwestern Colorado and northeastern Utah lies Brown's Park, along both sides of the river, and comprising an area approximately sixty miles long and from five to twenty miles in width. This is Colorado's western extremity of the vast cattle and sheep range which extends eastward one hundred and fifty miles, to the slopes of the Continental Divide. To the east and north of the Park is Cold Spring

11

Mountain, where sarvis berries grow in moist, shady nooks beneath the tall quaking aspens, and pine trees dot the mountain meadows with emerald islands. Westward is the forbidding wall of Diamond Mountain, with Wild Mountain alongside. Douglas Mountain on the south is bounded by the great canyon on the Green River, the entrance to which reminds one of Southey's poem, "How the water comes down at Lodore."

Major John Wesley Powell, the intrepid adventurer who first navigated the Green and Colorado Rivers from source to outlet, gave this canyon the name Lodore.

The lush valley of Brown's Hole attracted Indians, trappers and traders, prospectors and, later, settlers and outlaws. The Bassett family, among the first permanent settlers in Brown's Hole, remained as residents of the area for 120 years.

There are two versions as to how the area came to be known as Brown's Hole. Many historians believe the area was so named for a French Canadian trapper, Baptiste Brown, who arrived in 1830. Others believe the name was derived in honor of "Bible Back" Brown who also arrived early in the area and is said to have recommended the valley along the Green River as a good place to spend the harsh winter months. Jesse S. Hoy, one of the early settlers, didn't believe either account. He later wrote in his *History of Brown's Park*:

When we emerged from Red Creek Canyon that November day in 1872, looking east we could see the entire length and both sides of the Hole; two apparently unbroken mountain ranges, covered with a dense growth of low cedars and pinon, the whole representing a dark brown in appearance approaching black. The rocks also where they were visible, were a dark brown, so that we were all impressed with the same thought—the Hole was rightly named brown. All the stories told that it was named after a trapper by the name of Brown are pure fiction.

This historic marker indicates the site of Fort Davy Crockett in the Brown's Hole area. *Museum of Northwest Colorado*

In 1852, two rugged frontiersmen, Samuel Clark Bassett and Luther "Louis" Simmons, arrived in the area, fresh from the California gold rush of 1849. Simmons was the son-in-law of Kit Carson, the famed mountain man and scout. Carson had most likely attended the annual mountain man rendezvous held at Horse Creek near the Green River in 1833 and, according to his autobiography, he did attend the rendezvous at Green River in 1837. That same year three independent trappers, William Craig, Phillips Thompson, and a man named Sinclair, built a fort and trading post of adobe and cottonwood logs on the north bank of the Green River approximately three miles upstream from the gates of Lodore Canyon. The establishment was named Fort Davy Crockett in honor of the Texas frontiersman killed the previous year at the battle to defend the Alamo. It was also called Fort Misery by many of the soldiers stationed in the desolate area. The fort was the social center for the trappers, tradersand Ute Indians in the area. It was a hollow square compound with log cabins with dirt floors and dirt roofs, much as that of Fort William.

13

Famed scoutsman, Christopher "Kit" Carson hunted game for the fort for two years.
Denver Public Library

George Frederick Ruxton, who described Brown's Hole as a "mountain-walled valley," attended a mountain man rendezvous near the fort on the Green River. Ruxton later wrote of the experience in his memoirs, *Life in the Far West*: "Singly, and in bands numbering two to ten, the trappers dropped into the rendezvous, some with many pack loads of beaver."

Several trappers and traders passed through here including Robert Newell and Joseph C. Meek. Simmons had trapped in the area and attended the mountain man rendezvous of 1830, held at Brown's Hole. Simmons was smitten with the rugged beauty and isolation and returned the following year.

Sam Bassett was a former scout along the Overland Trail. He later served as a scout with Union General Nelson Miles during the Civil War. Following the war, Bassett returned to the area of Brown's Hole where he filed on a homestead and became one of the earliest pioneer settlers of Brown's Hole. Bassett kept a journal recording his thoughts of his westward travels. Only a few pages survive. The following quote from his journal was included in Ann Bassett's memoirs:

> Brown's Hole, November, the month of Thanksgiving, 1852. Louis [Simmons] and I "'down in." Packs off. Mules in lush cured meadow. Spanish Joe's trail for travel could

be likened to an 'up-state' high lane for coach-and-four. Mountains to the left of us, not in formation but highly mineralized. To the South, a range in uncontested beauty of contour, its great stone mouth drinking a river. Called on neighbors lest we jeopardize our social standing. Chief Catump, and his tribe of Utes. Male and female he created them. And Solomon in all his glory was not arrayed so fine. Beads, bones, quills, and feathers of artistic design. Buckskins tanned in exquisite coloring of amazing hues, resembling velvets of finest texture. Bows and arrows. "Let there be no strife between me and thee."

By this time, the fort had been abandoned and the old trail once used by trappers and traders was utilized by wandering prospectors, cowboys, rustlers, and outlaws. The area Ann Bassett described was the location of her Uncle Sam's first cabin in the area, near the entrance to Lodore Canyon, where the mighty Green River flows as it leaves the Brown's Hole area. He later built a log cabin on the west bank of Beaver Creek where the creek flows down from Cold Spring Mountain at the extreme northern edge of Brown's Hole. Here, Bassett brought in a few head of cattle and began a small ranch.

When Bassett made Brown's Hole his permanent home, there were no white women in the area. Bassett's diary entry, dated June 22, 1854, recounts his pleasure of the arrival of the first white woman: "Warren P. Parsons and his wife Annie have arrived, and our first white squaw, 'Snapping Annie,' is expertly driving her slick oxen 'Turk' and 'Lion.' 'Whoa! How, Turk! Gee, Lion!' commanded by a female bullwacker."

In her unpublished memoirs, Ann Bassett wrote: "Some writers have given the impression that there were white women in the Hole at an earlier date, at Camp Misery, [Fort Davy Crockett] the old fort in Dummies Bottom. Jim Baker and others reported no white women in the Hole until Snapping Annie Parsons [Laureate Ann] came."

Samuel Bassett Sr. and Anna Marie Scott met and were later married in Brownsville, Jefferson County, New York, in January 1832. There, Anna Marie gave birth to their first child, Amos Herbert, born July 31, 1834, Samuel Clark Bassett II followed two years later, on June 27, 1836. The family later moved to Menard County, Illinois, where the elder Bassett engaged in farming. Following their formal education, teenaged Sam eventually left the family farm, heading west for adventure and opportunity. Amos Herbert, known as

Lodore Canyon. *Museum of Northwest Colorado*

Herb, stayed on the farm, continued his education, graduated from college and became a teacher in the local community.

When the Civil War broke out, 28 year-old Herb Bassett volunteered for the Union Army. He was mustered in as a private, on August 14, 1862, at Athens, Illinois. He was assigned to serve in Company K of the 106th Regiment of "Lincoln's Brigade." Bassett, who was also a musician, joined the regiment's band with the official title of "Drummer." In 1863, barely a year into his service with the Union cause, Bassett fell ill. His Army records indicate the illness only as a "debility." He was sent home for a month of rest and rehabilitation. He later returned to his regiment

The Green River. *Museum of Northwest Colorado*

where he served admirably throughout the war.

Following the war, Major Amos Herbert Bassett was honorably discharged on July 12, 1865, at Pine Bluff, Arkansas. With his educational background, Bassett gained employment with the government, serving as Collector of Revenue at the port of Norfolk, Virginia. Through his government work, Herb Bassett met and became friends with many influential people, including the esteemed Judge Crawford Miller, a respectable judge in the Virginia district.

A few years later, Bassett asked Judge Miller for permission to court his granddaughter, the lovely and vivacious Mary Eliza Chamberlain Miller. Mary Eliza, along with a sister, Hannah, had been orphaned when they were young. They were living with their maternal grandparents when she met Bassett.

Not long after the courtship began, Bassett was forced to return to Arkansas where he continued his employment as Collector of Revenue. He later became Clerk of the District Court at Little Rock. However, his courtship with Elizabeth, as she was known, continued, albeit long distance.

17

Sam Bassett. *Museum of Northwest Colorado*

The marriage between Amos Herbert Bassett and Mary Eliza Chamberlain Miller took place in Hot Springs, Arkansas, on September 21, 1871. The groom was 37 years-old and the bride had just turned 16.

It was a marriage of opposites. While both Herb and Elizabeth were well educated, their personalities were very different. Herb was a quiet, reserved, and unassuming man, while Elizabeth was charming, outgoing, and personable, but was known to have quite a temper when provoked.

After their marriage, the newlyweds lived in Hot Springs, where Herb served as Clerk of the Court. Three years later Elizabeth gave birth to their first child, Josephine, in 1874. A son, Samuel, named for Herb's father and brother, was born two years later. Shortly after Samuel was born, Herb's health began to suffer. He later described his ailment in an application for an Army pension:

> Was treated in Arkansas 20 years ago for liver and heart trouble—had chills and fever frequently for several years after the war over—was treated by Dr. Henry C. Baker who stated that my liver was in very bad condition—that the chills and fever that I had were very hard to control. While he was treating me I had a very hard chill which threatened congestion and he advised me to leave there at once. I sold out and came here [Brown's Hole] in April 1878.

Due to his health and after years of coaxing by his brother Sam, Herb finally agreed with his younger brother to relocate to Brown's Hole. Elizabeth, high-spirited and adventurous, supported her husband's decision with great enthusiasm. Ann Bassett later wrote: "Later when my mother glimpsed the richly green, natural meadows, and the groves of stately, wide-branched cottonwoods, she was reminded of a beautiful park in the eastern land where she was born. At once she rechristened the lovely valley, 'Brown's Park.'"

However, J. S. Hoy, in his unpublished memoir, had a different recollection of how Brown's Hole became Brown's Park. Hoy wrote:

> In 1869 when Major Powell passed down the Green, he named things and places [he] thought worthy of a name, to suit his fancy which was both poetical and romantic. Brown's Hole grated upon his cultured ears so he changed it to Brown's Park, there [being] considerable difference between a hole and a park.
>
> Pot creek, on the mountains near the south of the Hole, running parallel with Green river he named Cascade creek. At the bottom of every cascade there is a hole, as water in this creek ran only a couple months in the spring-while the snow was melting-after which there were no cascades by many holes, so the denizens of the country continue to call it Pot creek.
>
> He named a park or hole just east of Lodore Canyon, Zenobia Basin, in honor of [a] semi-barbarian lady, who was [a] descendant of Jupiter and Queen of Palmyra and Egypt.
>
> Green river when leaving Brown's Hole cuts a way through the Uintah Mountains. The part or extension of this range east of Lodore Canyon is locally known as Douglas Mountains, the highest of which Powell named Zenobia Peak, it being about 8,000 feet above sea level, situated but a few miles east of Lodore Canyon.

Diamond mountain, north of Brown's Hole in Colorado, and opposite the mountain above described and about 40 miles apart, was named from being "salted" by the wild and get-rich-quick Arnold and gang of rascals.

Beaver Basin was named after Beaver creek and both were named after beaver of which there was an abundance in both at one time. The name Beaver Basin was changed during the 80's to Cold Spring Mountain, from the number of exceptionally cold springs there. Douglas Springs and Douglas Mountain were named after Chief Douglas of the White River Utes. This section was one of the principal winter resorts of deer and is where I engaged in what I have described as "the greatest deer hunt on record."

While Sam Bassett was certainly considered one of the earliest settlers in the rugged area, there were others who had arrived before Herb Bassett conceded to his brother's urging. During the winter of 1871-1872, George Baggs wintered a herd of his Texas cattle in Brown's Hole. It was an unusually harsh winter, with cattle perishing throughout the region. However, at Brown's Hole, that little green valley between the mountain ranges, Baggs's cattle survived the winter. Baggs gathered his 900 head that spring and herded them north, letting everyone know about the fertile area and mild climate of Brown's Hole. Back in Wyoming, Baggs sold his herd to a large cattle outfit.

That fall, James "Jesse" Smith Hoy was hired to drive a herd of cattle back to Brown's Hole for another winter's stay. Hoy liked the area and stayed, intending to build his own cattle empire in Brown's Hole.

Another early settler was Juan José Herrera. A native of Las Vegas, New Mexico, Herrera, along with a group of men including his brother, Pablo, had arrived in Brown's Hole in 1870. Soon dubbed "Mexican Joe" by the locals, Herrera's plan was to start his own cattle herd by rustling a few strays from the cattle owners whenever the opportunity presented itself.

Being a small, close-knit group of cattle owners, at least

The spectacular Brown's Park mountain range. *Museum of Northwest Colorado*

in the early years, word soon spread of Mexican Joe Herrera's bad reputation. Mexican Joe was a braggart, often telling anyone who would listen of killing three men in New Mexico. Herrera would also boast, after a few drinks, of his supposed distinguished Spanish ancestry. Not long after Herrera and his gang of rustlers had settled at the eastern end of the valley, not far from Sam Bassett's small claim, a few stray cattle were observed in Herrera's corral. On closer observation, some of these cattle were branded. Herrera had just returned from an unfortunate drinking spree in a saloon near South Pass, Wyoming, where he shot a man in the foot. Unfortunately, the man developed blood poisoning and soon died. Knowing there was a price on his head, Herrera sent for his old Wyoming friend, attorney Asbury B. Conway of South Pass, Wyoming, who arrived in 1871. Safe in Brown's Hole, nothing ever came of the murder charge but the locals knew there was a bad man residing in their otherwise peaceful area. Thus, Juan José "Mexican Joe" Herrera is known in the history of Brown's Hole, as the first known outlaw to reside in the area.

Nevertheless, Conway remained in Brown's Hole with Herrera and his gang of thieves. The 34- year-old attorney, a graduate of Iowa's University Law School, had arrived in South

This view, at the opposite end of the park, reveals why the rugged, isolated area appealed to outlaws. *Museum of Northwest Colorado*

Pass City in 1869 to prospect for gold and practice law. Finding neither gold nor profit in his law practice, Conway succumbed to his habit of heavy drinking. On the few occasions when Conway wasn't inebriated, he rode with Mexican Joe Herrera and his gang of cattle rustlers. J. S. Hoy, who had arrived in the Hole in December 1872, later wrote that Conway, along with Mexican Joe Herrera: "Scoured the country looking for cattle that had strayed from, or had been stolen from, the herds going to the northwest."

During the winter of 1872-1873, Mexican Joe and his gang stole livestock, food and whatever else they could from the few residents in Brown's Hole. However, when they arrived at Hoy's place, located near a bend of the Green River, they were met by Hoy and his shotgun. The gang backed off but Mexican Joe never forgot the humiliating encounter. J. S. Hoy didn't forget, either. The incident caused bad blood between the two, blood that would soon spill in violence.

Hoy, who would later be joined by his four brothers, established a cattle ranch in an area of Brown's Hole known as the "Bottoms." J. S. Hoy explained the area as, "This bottom was subject to overflow from high water in the Green." The first of his brothers, Valentine Shade, arrived, as J. S. Hoy later recounted: "October 4, 1873, my brother Valentine, George Spicer and his brother S. F. [Sam] Spicer arrived in the Hole with about 300 cattle."

The Hoy brothers would later become one of the many cattle baron operations detested by both Elizabeth Bassett and her daughter, Anna. J. S. Hoy described the area, where he first settled:

> The flies, mosquitoes, and gnats drove men and beasts to desperation. There was no relief from them night and day. The green-headed flies swarmed like bees while the sun was hot; the air was filled with their buzzing. They bunched the cattle that stood most of the day huddled together, stamping, rubbing against it over their backs. I have seen horses roll in the tall grass and groan in misery, unable to escape their innumerable tormentors. As the air cooled, the flies settled on the ground or in the grass, and mosquitoes arose in myriads to take their place. When it got too cold for the green-heads and mosquitoes the little buffalo gnats got in their work the remainder of the night.

In the spring of 1873, J. S. Hoy and his brother Valentine were in Wyoming purchasing cattle. Mexican Joe and his gang of thieves arrived at the Hoy ranch. With scythes in hand, the men proceeded to cut a considerable amount of hay along the river bottom which they then bundled and placed in Hoy's corral. Following the return of the Hoy brothers, Mexican Joe paid them a visit, demanding fifteen dollars per bundle for the hay he and his men had cut. J. S. Hoy refused to pay, again with his shotgun handy. Again, Mexican Joe left humiliated by Hoy. Not long after this incident, Hoy suspected that one of his missing steers had been stolen by Mexican Joe and his gang. Hoy rode boldly to the small ranch of the Herrera brothers, intending to inspect the brands of the cattle in Herrera's corral. When Hoy arrived and stated his purpose, Mexican Joe was outraged. J. S. Hoy described the scene:

If a bomb had been thrown in their cabin and exploded, it could not have created greater consternation and call to arms; a worse insult could not have been offered Joe or any other horse or cattle thief. They surrounded me chattering and jabbering in their own language, of which I understood but little, Joe saying; "You think me steal, eh? Examine the hides! Look more! Here is another one," and like exclamations. He fairly danced in his rage, while his eyes scintillated steel and lightning.

Then, Mexican Joe pulled his knife. Brandishing it in threatening manner in Hoy's direction, the sight of the large knife, Hoy later recalled: "had a tendency to make cold chills run up and down one's back, and gooseflesh crawl." Just as Mexican Joe made his move, knife in hand, toward Hoy, A. B. Conway rushed forward and shoved Mexican Joe aside. After a heated discussion, Hoy was allowed to leave. Hoy continued with his account: "After bearing the mental strain as long as I could, I concluded discretion was the better part of valor, and without telling anyone my intentions, I started back for my old camp on Bear River."

Evidently, with J. S. Hoy temporarily out of the area, Mexican Joe and his gang thought it was safe to steal more of Hoy's cattle. They hadn't counted on a run-in with Valentine S. Hoy. Hoy tracked down Mexican Joe at Jim Goodson's cabin on Willow Creek. When Hoy accused Mexican Joe of stealing his cattle, naturally a fight broke out. As Mexican Joe, with knife raised high, rushed Hoy, Hoy met him and ducked under Mexican Joe's arm. Swinging his adversary around, Hoy threw a punch which landed squarely on Mexican Joe's jaw. Mexican Joe landed face down on the dirt floor. Standing over the fallen man, Hoy pulled his own knife from a sheath in his boot. J. S. Hoy recounted what happened next: "Hoy aimed with one slash to rip Mexican Joe from end to end. As the blow was descending, two or three men caught his arm so that the blow only split one of Joe's buttocks. This laid Joe up for a month or two."

Eventually A. B. Conway found his sobriety and the error

of his ways. In the later part of 1874, Conway severed his ties with the Herrera gang and moved to Green River City, Wyoming. After operating a successful law practice for a number of years, Conway entered politics. J. S. Hoy saved a newspaper clipping [publication unknown] which read as follows: "In the election of state officers held on September 11, 1890, the onetime horse thief and cattle rustler was named a justice of the Supreme Court." A. B. Conway later became Chief Justice of the Wyoming Supreme Court in 1897, but died that same year, at the age of 60.

In the meantime, more and more settlers were entering the area. J. S. Hoy later recalled the settlers of Brown's Hole:

> 1876 witnessed the coming of a dozen or more men and women, nearly all of them locating at the upper end of Brown's Hole, in Utah, becoming citizens of the Hole. Among the most prominent were Jimmie Reed with his Indian wife Margaret. They built a cabin on the south side of Green river at the north of a creek that had its source near Pot creek and emptied into the Green, named at the time Jimmie Reed creek. W. B. Tittsworth came in the fall of 1876 and built a cabin on Green river opposite the Dr. Parson's cabin.
>
> E. H. Rife and C. B. Sears came with their wives from Denver and located on Pot creek.
>
> Frank Orr and Hank Ford came in 1876, as did Charles Crouse and Aaron Overholt, James L. Warren and Doctor Parsons. Others that may be classed as first settlers who came to Brown's Hole between 1876 and 1880 were: G. W. Edwards and his brother J. G. Edwards, George, James and Walter Scriyner, Tom Davenport, Tommy Dowdle, Frank Goodman, Harry Hindle, all Englishmen, John Jarvie, and George Law, Scotchmen.
>
> The above eleven drifted into the Hole from Rock Springs, Wyoming.
>
> A. H. Bassett with his wife came in 1878, their daughter Ann being the first child born in Brown's Hole.

In the spring of 1877, Herb Bassett brought his wife, Elizabeth, and their two small children, Josephine and Samuel, to Brown's Hole. Herb and his family stayed for a time in Sam's cabin, while Herb looked for work suitable with his previous work experience. In Evanston, Wyoming, Herb Bassett found work as a bookkeeper for a mercantile firm, A. C. Beckwith and Company. He also taught school in Green River City. However, as Elizabeth was pregnant with their third child, neither occupation provided enough income for Bassett to support his growing family.

Herb Bassett decided the family would homestead in Brown's Hole. In April 1878, once again he relied on his brother Sam, who guided the family's two wagons full of their possessions including Herb's beloved organ and treasured books, back to Brown's Hole. Sam took the only access road into Brown's Hole from the north which ran through Irish Canyon and down into Brown's Hole.

Josephine Bassett, the oldest child of Amos Herbert and Elizabeth Bassett, was four years-old when her parents and younger brother, Samuel, made that trip back to settle at Brown's Hole. Josie, as everyone called her, later spoke of the journey:

> We landed in Green River City. You see, there was no roads to Brown's Park [Hole] from Rock Springs at the time. We come over the mountains to Green River City to Brown's Park [Hole] with teams and wagons. One team was oxen, two steers. I'll never forget it in the world. I loved those cattle, but when they were unhitched, I was afraid of them. I would run and get upon that wagon and ride with the steers everytime, you know I was terribly scared.
>
> I don't know how many days we were in coming–I just barely can remember it. I was four years-old. And one reason I remember it so well, they had a team of oxen, and wasn't I afraid of those oxen! Oh! But I rode with them–I rode with Uncle Sam Bassett and his oxen all the way. But when I was on the ground I wasn't with them, I was someplace else. And that's how I come to remember our trip so well.

Ironically, it was at the suggestion of the outlaw, Mexican Joe, that Herb decided to settle at a place called Joe's Spring. Herb, Elizabeth, and the children stayed with Herb's brother Sam, in his small log cabin, located a few miles north of Lodore Canyon. Josie described her uncle's cabin as, "a funny little old log cabin with two rooms, no floors and no windows." The two Bassett brothers built a cabin for Herb and his growing family, as Elizabeth was in the final trimester of her pregnancy with the couple's third child. However, the new cabin was not completed by the time Elizabeth went into labor. Her daughter Anna was coming, ready or not.

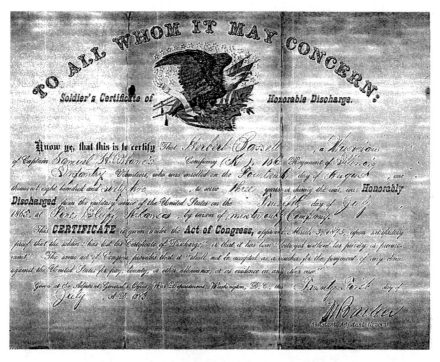

Herbert Bassett's Certificate of Honorable Discharge.
Museum of Northwest Colorado

CHAPTER NOTES AND SOURCE INFORMATION

The best source for the early history of Brown's Hole is *Where the Old West Stayed Young*, by John Rolfe Burroughs.

The Bureau of Land Management's 1982 publication of *An Isolated Empire: A History of Northwestern Colorado*, by Frederic J. Athearn, was also quite helpful.

Over time, the original spelling of "Ladore" has been changed to "Lodore."

The last mountain man rendezvous on the Green River occurred in 1840.

Ann Bassett Willis wrote of her life experiences in a four-part series published in the Colorado Historical Society's *Colorado Magazine*. The series titled, "Queen Ann of Brown's Park," ran in Volume XXIX January 1952, Volume XXIX April 1952, Volume XXIX October 1952, Volume XXX January 1953. They are available at the Denver Public Library. Unless otherwise noted, the quotes attributed to Ann are from this work.

The records of Private Amos Herbert Bassett are found in the United States National Archives.

James "Jesse" S. Hoy's quotes can be found in the J. S. Hoy manuscript, located at the Colorado History Center.

The "Bottoms," the area where the Hoy brothers first settled, is known today as the "Hoy Bottoms."

J. S. Hoy's comments regarding the early settlers is from his unpublished manuscript, *Early History of Brown's Hole*, courtesy Valentine Hoy IV.

The Bassett family arrived in Brown's Hole in 1877, but returned permanently in 1878.

It should be noted that in Ann's working memoir, *Scars and Two Bars*, an excerpt of which was printed in the April 1, 1943, issue of the *Moffat County Mirror*, Ann's year of birth is given as 1875, two years before Herb and Elizabeth first arrived in Brown's Hole. It is not known if this was Ann's error or a typo by the editor of the newspaper. In any case, it is obviously an error.

In 1960 and 1961, Josephine Bassett McKnight Ranney Williams Wells Morris gave a series of taped interviews. The particular quotes in this chapter are from the interviews conducted by Murl Messersmith, July 6, 1961. Dinosaur National Monument, Jensen, Utah. Typewritten account available at the Museum of Northwest Colorado, Craig, Colorado.

The early Bassett Ranch. *Museum of Northwest Colorado*

The Bassett cattle herd. *Museum of Northwest Colorado*

BIRTH OF A CATTLE QUEEN

It was in Sam Bassett's tiny cabin where on May 12, 1878, Elizabeth, attended by another new settler, Doctor John D. Parsons, gave birth to her third child, Anna Marie, named for her paternal grandmother. Anna Bassett was the first white child to be born not only in Brown's Hole, but all of northwestern Colorado. Ann's older sister, Josie later recalled: "My sister Ann was born in May after we got there [Brown's Hole] in March. She was born May 12. And I tell you, my sister was a curiosity; a baby in Brown's Park. Old trappers and old mountaineers of all kinds came to see the baby."

Elizabeth could not nurse baby Anna, so local ranchers came to the aid of the Bassett family, finding an Indian woman who agreed to serve as a wet nurse. Elizabeth was so grateful to the Ute Indians she spent as much time with them as she could, engaging in long conversations. The Utes enjoyed her warm presence and caring nature as well as her dialog with them. They called her "Magpie," a name she was proud of. Anna, who preferred to be called "Ann," recounted the story of her birth later in her memoirs, as supposedly related to her by her parents:

> A troop of Ute Indians were camped about two hundred yards from the cabin, among these was an Indian mother, See-a-baka, who had a new-born papoose. Buffalo Jack Rife, good old "'Buff,'" spoke their language like a Ute, so after consultation with Dr. Parsons (this elderly doctor died the next year, to everyone's sadness, since there never again was to be a medical man in residence) he held a pow-wow with Chief Marcisco and Medicine Man Mush-qua-gant Star.' After making considerable medicine and sign talk,

it was decided to permit the squaw to become my wet nurse and me to become a foster twin to her papoose, a boy named Kab-a-weep, meaning Sunrise. Indians do not coddle newborn infants by covering the head. I've been told it was storming when they carried me to the Indian wickiup, and I can imagine how I must have blinked and grimaced as the snow settled on my little face. It was the custom of the Indians to move from the river bottoms where they wintered, to cooler summer camp grounds on the mountain tops. For that reason my Uncle Sam built the "double-cabins" for mother at the head of Willow Creek, so she could be near my foster mother. To this cabin See-a-baka came at regular intervals to feed me. I nursed for six months, until cow's milk could be provided. It was Judge Conway who rounded up a milk cow and presented her to me, so I got into the cow business at a decidedly early age.

The milk cow was not only a blessing to the Bassett family, but the beginning of their eventual cattle herd. The Army pension Herb received monthly was of great assistance to the struggling family as they built their new life in the West. Herb, with the assistance of friendly neighbors, built a five-room single-story log home for his family. However, during the construction of the home, the children, Samuel, Josie, and baby Ann, broke out with measles. Elizabeth set up comfortable bedding under the cottonwood trees where they could rest in the fresh air. True to her pioneer spirit and character, she kept one eye on the children while helping her husband hew the logs for the cabin. Elizabeth, a lively southern belle, was entirely up to the challenges of this new frontier.

On the other hand, Herb Bassett was a man out of place in the rugged Brown's Park frontier. He was well-read and very musical, as well as a scholar, which was not compatible with hard physical outdoor labor. Yet he persevered in the true pioneer spirit. Ann later described the new log cabin and the home decor:

There was a big cook stove, innumerable iron pots and brass kettles, feather beds, several "spool" beds. All these shipped from Grandfather's Virginia plantation and hauled to the ranch in wagons. He [Herb Bassett] became resolutely set against hauling any more "boughten" house furnishings. Birch grew in profusion along all the streams. Rawhide was plentiful. Father solved our problems by making small tables and chairs using birch for the frames, and rawhide strips for seats and backs. Cushions were made of buckskin filled with milkweed floss. The curtain problem was made for mother to solve. She traded Indian Mary ten pounds of sugar for a bale of fringed buckskins. Father fashioned curtain rings from the leg bones of deer, and thus we made drapes for the windows.

Ann continued her description:

The home contained good books such as Shakespeare's complete works, Shelley, Keats, Dickens, Byron, Longfellow, and many other works of poems, literature, and travel. My parents had brought books from their eastern home. Others were given us by Judge Conway. Bassett's ranch was a place for people to congregate, relax and read.

Most important was the large cook stove—built to last not to lift. There were a few choice pieces of china for which we had no use for.

The land on which Herb built his home was open on the south end and sheltered by the hills on the other three sides. A gentle flowing stream of cold mountain water wandered its way through the homestead. Across the valley was the site of Lodore Canyon. Herb planted a vegetable garden and Elizabeth, with a strong determination to succeed in this western land, began buying Durham cattle. Josie later recalled: "My father didn't know how to brand a cow—neither did she, [Elizabeth] but she tried."

While the Bassett family, Samuel and later, his brother, Amos Elbert, are considered to be among the first settlers in the area, others soon followed. Ann later described the pioneers who also settled in the region:

Dr. and Mrs. Parsons put up a cozy cabin on the banks of Green River at Parson's Ford. Jimmie and Mary Jane Goodson selected ranches on Willow Creek. John Jarvie and pretty Nell built a trading post and established the first Post Office. Tom Davenport and gentle Alice, who mothered the entire community, started cattle ranches on Willow Creek. Ed Rife and Genevieve built up the Crittenden Horse Company, bred the best of stock and were citizens any country would claim with pride. Whitcombe W. James and Jennie—our school teacher, who had a high regard for consistency—made their home close to Green River. Frank and Elizabeth Goodman, considerate, estimable folks, engaged in sheep ranching. C. B. Sears and his wife Molly were examples of good citizenship, who also were in the sheep business. James Warren had been educated for the priesthood, but found cattle ranching more to his inclination. His devoted wife, Katherine, cared for the sick with skill and kindness. Charles Allen and Lizzie located their ranch on the Green River meadows, where her sweet voice and cheerful disposition were an inspiration to her neighbors. Charley Crouse specialized in thoroughbred horses, and never will I forget those splendid animals with their arched, glossy necks and dark, fiery eyes. Mary Crouse was surely the "salt of the earth," a gracious and beautiful woman.

During the Ute Indian uprising which culminated with the Meeker Massacre in 1879, the Bassett family, along with several other small ranchers in the area, left Brown's Hole for their safety. When the Bassett's returned, Herb and Elizabeth were shocked to find that several head of cattle were missing. Josie described the situation:

My father bought twenty head of heifers just before the Meeker Massacre and he branded his heifers with "U P" on the ribs. Great big "U" with the "P" connected. But while we were away in Wyoming a man came into the country, his name was Metcalf...and he branded with "7 U P." He had a "7" in front of our "U P" all over those cows. My father didn't know what to do, he was stranded–but my mother did. She said, "I know some of those cows, and I'm taking them." And she took them! She and Mr. Metcalf had some kind of set-with [and] she didn't use "U P" anymore, she had the cattle rebranded.

During that year of 1879, Herb's health had improved dramatically. In 1879, Herb and "Buffalo" Jack Rife built a cabin in Zenobia Basin. Again, Ann related the details of her father's cabin: "Father cut logs, dragged them to the site by saddle horse, and hewed timbers for the door facings and floors for a three room cabin which still stands intact."

The cabin was in a grassy meadow at the base of Douglas Mountain, several miles from the ranch, where Herb intended to move the cattle for the summer months. Before the herd was moved, the cattle were branded. The Bassett brand was the Zee Bar Kay. Z-K was branded on the left side of the animals, while the left ear was split and the right ear was cropped.

While Herb did his fair share in the family cattle enterprise, it was Elizabeth who operated the ranch. She worked with the cattle, kept an eye out for any roaming animals, participated in the branding, and learned to use a rifle and shotgun. She rode the fence line daily and surveyed her land on horseback. Herb strung four-stranded barbed wire around his property, the first rancher to do so in Brown's Hole. Later, Herb, with the help of Tom Davenport, was the first to grow grain in the area and bought cradles and scythes used to harvest the grain for feeding the animals.

In addition to the cattle, Herb and Elizabeth began raising thoroughbred horses. This was a great desire of Elizabeth, the granddaughter of a great breeder of fine horses in Virginia. Elizabeth soon gained a local reputation as a respectable breeder of her thoroughbreds. Esther Anderson Campbell bought one of the Bassett's horses. Esther and Ann became close friends. Esther later described the day young Ann Bassett first saw Campbell's buckskin horse, recognizing it as one from her mother's stock.

They owned the original mare, the 'Tippecanoe' mare, and raised many good colts from her. Her father [Herb] bought the mare from some people traveling through the country from Tennessee. She was high-lifted and they had a wire tied around her tongue to control her. Her tongue was almost cut in two. Mr. Bassett felt sorry for her and bought her. Her colts were always full of life and willing to travel. Ann had a team of buckskins for a buggy wagon. She drove them from Douglas to Craig from sunup to sundown, and they would be pulling at the bits when they trotted up the last hill to Craig.

Herb and Elizabeth both believed in raising their children to help on the family ranch. At a very early age, the Bassett boys, Samuel, Elbert, and George, all learned to rope and ride and were given their chores on the ranch. Both Elbert and George were born in Brown's Hole, Elbert was born June 21, 1880, and George was born March 29, 1884.

The strong-willed Elizabeth insisted her two daughters, Josie and Ann, learn the same ranching skills. Ann later described the chores that went with a working ranch:

We had to work. Horses, cattle, or sheep, as the case might be, required constant care. The farming, raising and "putting up" hay was a part time job. Our system of living depended on individual productive industry for its well being. Staple groceries and clothing had to be hauled from Rock Springs, Wyoming, by wagons over rough roads, a hundred miles away. It required about ten days to complete the round trip. This was done spring and fall.

All farming was done the first few years. There were only a few plows in the country. These plows, as were other farming equipment, were used or loaned all around the area where needed. Grain was threshed by driving horses over the bundles placed on the ground in clean swept corrals, and cleaned of chaff by a home made fanning mill.

Elizabeth raised her daughters to be strong and independent in the rugged, isolated area of Brown's Hole. Both girls were accomplished horsewomen at a very young age. Being a sophisticated southern woman, Elizabeth rode sidesaddle and always in a dress. Both Josie and Ann preferred riding their horses as their father and brothers did, and wearing pants. Ann greatly admired the accomplishments and character of her mother. She later wrote, "Mother was a natural executive as well as an excellent horsewoman." She also commented on her mother's riding habits: "Her outfit consisted of a beautifully fitted 'habit' of rich, dark blue material, long-skirted and draped with grace. For trimming, there were a number of gleaming brass buttons. She was a blonde. Mounted on her thoroughbred horse, 'Calky,' she was a picture to remember."

As Elizabeth enlarged her cattle herd and horse-breeding enterprise, she also grew more independent. She was a woman with a wide range of interests. So taken with her new life in the West, she became enamored with the area and the people. She loved the land and hated the name of Brown's Hole. Elizabeth began a crusade to officially change the name of Brown's Hole to Brown's Park. Her efforts succeeded when the official post office of Brown's Park was established on February 14, 1881. The post office was located on the John Jarvie ranch, one of the first settlers in the area. Jarvie served as postmaster, followed by Herb Bassett in January 1890.

In time, the Brown's Hole early era of the mountain men and explorers gave way to the Brown's Park era of settlers and cattle ranchers. These pioneers of Brown's Park formed a tight-knit caring community. Due to the isolation, rugged area, and harsh conditions, it was human nature as well as a necessity. When the only doctor in the area, John D. Parsons, who had delivered Ann, died in 1881, Elizabeth served the Brown's Park area as the community doctor. Ann recounted one of the many occasions where her mother's services were required:

37

One young man of our neighborhood was riding near a barbed wire fence and his horse ran into the wire, which cut the flesh of the cowpuncher's leg to the bone. It was a deep, bad cut. Mother was called as usual. She put five stitches into the flesh, with sewing or sack needles as used on horses and cattle, with common table salt as an antiseptic, and herbs gathered by the Indians to stop the flow of blood.

While Elizabeth lent her medical skills for the good of the community, Herb established what would become the first public school district in northwest Colorado. Four students attended the first school term in 1881, held in the dugout home of Henry and Jennie Jaynes. The students included the two Jaynes children and the older Bassett children, Josie and Sam. Josie later recalled:

In winter, of course, we had to go to school. I can remember when we only had three months school. There was no district organized in having school, my father was trying hard to have a district. And there was only a few children. I went, but I wasn't old enough. I wasn't hardly school age, had to be seven years old then, and I wasn't. But I went and drew public money just the same 'cause there had to be so many from a district to have a school district organized. Well school was taught just over the rise towards the river, just directly between the river and the school house that is there now. Mrs. Jaynes was the teacher.

With a school district now established and public money being available, the new teacher, Mrs. Jennie Jaynes, was able to earn a small salary. Ann would later write:

A meeting was called resulting in an agreement to collect an additional sum to pay a teacher a few months each year. The dug out was built by donated work on the Harry Hoy ranch at Sears Draw, and there Mrs. Jaynes taught Brown's Park children. Seven pupils, Josie Bassett, Joe Davenport, Willis Rouff, Joseph Jaynes and the three Reed children,

Jimmie, Ella and Charles. The Reeds were half Indian children.

Ann and her younger brothers would later attend the same school, improved by the construction of a fine log building. Education of his children was a priority to Herb Bassett. The earliest public record of the Bassett children's educational development appeared in an early Craig newspaper, the *Colorado Pantograph*, printed in a November, 1892, issue. "The Misses Bassett and Mr. Matt Rash arrived in the city Monday from Brown's Park. The young ladies are here for the purpose of attending school, and are stopping at the home of Mr. Joe Carroll."

As the Bassett cattle ranch began to show a profit, improvements were made on the property. Barns were built, as well as a corral for the horses. A bunkhouse for hired help was erected. Herb piped the spring to bring the water closer to the log home and to provide irrigation for the garden. He established hay fields, becoming the first man in the Park to do so, providing winter forage for the cattle and horses.

Herb and Elizabeth Bassett were well known in Brown's Park for their hospitality to guests and generosity and kindness to their hired hands. With Elizabeth's outgoing nature and Herb's ability to entertain with music and intelligent conversation, the Bassett ranch became the social hub of Brown's Park. Ann Bassett would later describe the Bassett ranch:

> Our ranch became the accepted stopping place for travelers entering Brown's Park. Quantities of good food was provided. Music was furnished and the gaieties lasted for several days and nights. Mrs. Davenport, Mrs. Jarvie and Mrs. Allen possessed beautiful voices and they sang many of the old songs. Many of the older men were chess addicts, and whiled away a few hours at that pastime.

Josie remembered the Christmas seasons with great affection. She later said:

Mr. and Mrs. Charles Sparks *Museum of Northwest Colorado*

We had a Christmas tree. My mother was great on having
a Christmas tree and homemade candy and popcorn,
and peanuts. And you know, they strung the berries from
the wild rose bushes to decorate the tree. I strung many
of them. [We] had a Christmas tree for all the children.
You know the old time cowboys took an interest in that.
That was a kind of curiosity to them. Some fellows I can
remember came there and enjoyed that Christmas tree just
as well as the children. Mother would bake pies and cookies
and a lot of things. We had supper, sometimes they danced.
I can remember when our house had dirt floors and father
hewed a cottonwood log.

The Bassetts had made good friends in the Hole, and
all were welcomed at their home, including Judge Conway, the
Jarvies, Charlie Sparks, Charlie and Mary Crouse, and, for awhile,
Valentine Shade Hoy. However, as events turned out, Hoy and his

four brothers, James Jesse Smith, Adea A., Benjamin Frank, and Harry (Henry) did not consider themselves friends of the Bassetts, or any of the other small ranchers, for that matter.

As previously mentioned, James "Jesse" Smith Hoy (he was known as Jesse) first arrived in the area in December 1872. He trailed a herd of cattle for the Crawford-Thompson Cattle Company south from Evanston, Wyoming, into the north end of Brown's Hole. Here, he built a cabin, and stayed with the cattle through the winter. He remained in the area, receiving another herd of Crawford-Thompson cattle the following year. In 1873 his brother Valentine drove 300 head of cattle from Greeley, Colorado, to Brown's Hole, joining his brother. Jesse S. Hoy left Brown's Hole for a time, returning to Evanston, after a violent confrontation with the fellow known as "Mexican Joe." After serving a two-year term in the Wyoming Territorial Legislature, he returned to Brown's Hole, joining three of his brothers Valentine, Benjamin and Adea, both of whom arrived in 1875. Harry joined his brothers in 1880.

The five Hoy brothers, hailing from an influential and

Mr. and Mrs. Charles Crouse
Museum of Northwest Colorado

wealthy family at Hoy Gap, Pennsylvania, used much of the family wealth to begin five individual ranches in the newly named Brown's Park. Rumors ran throughout the Park that the Hoy brothers were bent on spreading their cattle operations and taking over the area. Incredible as it may seem, in 1884 a state survey was conducted, as it was unclear exactly where the Colorado state line ended and the Utah state line began in the western mountainous hills of Brown's Park. Following the survey, the state of Colorado allowed the homesteaders to file for clear title of their land. Herb Bassett immediately traveled to Hahn's Peak, the county seat of Routt County, near Steamboat Springs, officially to record his homestead on September 22, 1884.

Other residents of Brown's Park unfortunately either delayed or did not officially record their land claims. Valentine S. Hoy in a circuitous, underhanded action, also went to Hahn's Peak, filing on the land that several homesteaders had not officially recorded. This undermining scheme by Hoy caused outrage among the ranchers in the Park. Many of the early settlers were forced to leave the area, and those that remained, including Herb Bassett, never forgave the Hoy brothers for the devious treachery. Ann's older sister, Josie, recalled this episode in a one of her many taped interviews:

> The Hoys came first and tried to make a monopoly of everything. V. S. Hoy wasn't a good man. You see, when the survey was made, V. S. Hoy was a smart man...all the Hoys were. V. S. Hoy was the cook with the survey party. He had a nice business, he was there for a purpose. Now he knew the numbers of places and put swift on them, bought the land, and what he didn't buy with swift he had people coming here from Fremont, Nebraska and Leavenworth, Kansas to take up homesteads. Then he met them at Glenwood Springs, where they'd take up proof, paid them each a thousand dollars and they were gone. He had their homes and that's how the Hoys got all of the Hoy bottoms. He tried to swift my father's place, but my father's filing on the homestead had gone in just before his swift got there, so

that didn't work. My father never liked the Hoys, that made a bad spot. My dad was a very forgiving man but he never forgave that, no sir! He said, "I've been a friend to V. S. Hoy and thought he was a friend to me, and to have him do that–I'll have nothing to with him." And he never did.

Years later, J. S. Hoy had a decidedly different, if not arrogant, view of those early years in Brown's Park:

So far as I know, covering a period of fifty or more years, I have never known a single instance where cattlemen ever tried to or did drive an honest man or honest homesteader off the range. On the contrary, cattlemen big and little, rather invited men, poor men to live in their midst, helped them in various ways. As owners usually had plenty other work to do, and cowboys had a decided repugnance to engage in farming, they encouraged the "poor man" to homestead; gave them employment at times, such as freighting in supplies, helping make hay, bought their hay, grain and vegetables, and at times gave them beef and other provisions without charge when they were in need.

Nevertheless, the Hoy brothers lost the respect of many citizens of Brown's Park. Perhaps their disdain for Hoy's actions and the fall-out of those actions can best be summarized as follows: "The Hoys, with family money to invest, had ambitions of setting up a range empire, but found themselves so hedged in by other outfits and belligerent homesteaders that they had to content themselves with relatively modest spreads."

Despite the Hoy brothers attempt to illegally buy out the smaller ranch owners, other large cattle operations moved into Brown's Park with like intentions of taking over the best cattle-grazing land. The Middlesex Cattle Company was one such operation. The company, financed by Boston interests, located their operation just north and west of Brown's Park. The local manager, John Clay, intended to build a large cattle empire. Among the several cattle brands they registered, one brand, known as the

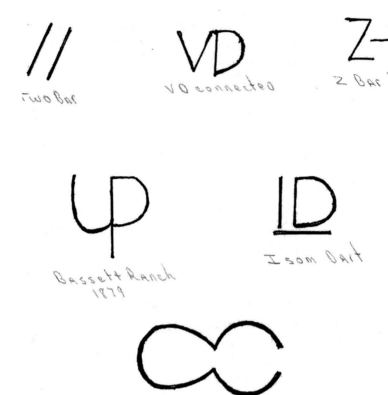

Cattle Brands. *Linda Wommack*

"VD Connected" or "Flying Vee Dee," commonly referred as "VD" cattle, soon became known throughout Brown's Park. Clay threatened to "buy all the 'little fellows' out or drive them out of the country." J. S. Hoy later recounted:

> The great Cattle Boom of the early eighties was at this time beginning. To be known as a cattleman was all that was needed to give one prestige and credit. Greedy [men] scanned the ranges from horizon to horizon looking for unoccupied country upon which to turn herds of cattle. An outfit known as the Middlesex Cattle Company, a millionaire company whose home office was in Boston, Massachusetts, sent agents into the Brown's Hole country.

They paid Jack Gunn fifty-five thousand dollars for his buildings; offered Spicer forty thousand for his cattle; offered the Hoys one hundred and twenty-five thousand dollars for theirs along with the threat that they would buy all the "little fellows" out or drive them out of the country.

Noder and Steadman and Jack Gunn were the only ones who sold to this greedy octopus. These two outfits were wise, the rest of us were foolish that we did not sell. This big company or corporation continued to use Gunn's brand – the letter G.

Jack Gunn had moved his herd of Texas cattle north of Brown's Hole, near the headwaters of Beaver Creek in the fall of 1879. In Ann's memoirs, she recounted the incident:

Jack's cattle, supplemented by the herds of the settlers in Brown's Park, were the only users of the range until the Middlesex outfit, who controlled the greater part of southwestern Wyoming, began to move their herds southward, and they came like a flood, devouring and consuming everything in their path. When they reached Beaver Basin, Jack Gun saw that it was useless for him to stand alone with his small herd against the thousands and thousands of cattle being pushed onward and southward.

When the Middlesex Cattle Company began their encroachment into Brown's Park, the ranchers held firm, with only two ranchers selling out to the corporate cattle company. Five year-old Ann found herself in the middle of a misunderstanding regarding Middlesex company policy when she found a sickly stray calf. The manager of the Middlesex Cattle Company, which owned the calf, gave the animal to little Ann, which carried the Middlesex brand. Ann brought the animal home, and her tender care and complete attention saved the calf's life. Later, a roving Middlesex cowboy spotted the calf and returned it to the Middlesex herd. Eight year-old Ann confronted the manager of the Middlesex Company with great determination demanding her given cow be returned to her. Retrieving her animal, she took it back to the Bassett ranch, and immediately persuaded one of the ranch wranglers to alter the brand on the cow. It was her first experience at a rumored career of cattle rustling that would remain throughout her life, and may have been the driving force that later gained her fame as she fought against the large cattle companies. Ann later wrote of this childhood event:

A mother cow never forgets where she puts her calf and will return from a long distance to find it. If for any reason the cow is unable to return and the little calf manages to dodge the coyotes, it becomes a "dogie," a name given to orphan calves.

In the spring of 1883 I found a dogie that was left by the mother when the drive passed our ranch. This calf had wandered into our pasture and located itself near a clump of protective willows where it could nip the soft green grass.

But it required milk, it could not live entirely on grass, and was about at the folding-up stage when I found it. The wild little brute was full of fight, but I managed to get it to the house, over a distance of a mile, which took most of the day and a lot of relays.

After I fed the calf milk-a forced feeding-I went to Mother and told her about my find. When she saw the starved, tiny creature that had been branded and ear-marked at that tender age, she immediately made it clear to me that I could feed and care for the calf, but as soon as it could eat grass and grew strong enough to rustle its living without milk, I must turn it on the range. The calf of the long horned Texas breed, covered with burrs and emaciated from starvation, was not a very promising looking critter.

With constant attention and kindness it learned to drink milk, and started to grow into something resembling a calf. I decided that I never would give the precious creature up, such a thing was unthinkable, for the little waif was as fond of me as I was of it.

Calf branding at the Charlie Sparks ranch. Ann's friend, Rosalie Miles is the gloved woman second from left. *Uintah County Libary, Vernal, Utah*

All over the tri-state area of Colorado, Utah, and Wyoming, the large corporate cattle ranches were ruthless and did everything legal, and even illegal, to acquire good ranch land in Brown's Park. Several ranchers reported stolen cattle, including the Bassett ranch. Herb strung barbed wire fencing around his land, the first in the Park to do so.

Elizabeth finally had enough of the large cattle companies threatening her and the other ranchers of Brown's Park. With her charm and keen business sense, she was able to hire Isom Dart, a former slave, and Madison Matthew (Matt) Rash, both of whom were former employees of the Middlesex Cattle Company, and Jack Fitch, a friend of Dart. Other hired ranch hands included Angus McDougall and James (Jim) Fielding McKnight. While Matt Rash worked for the Bassett ranch, he had acquired his own piece of land some two miles west of the Bassett ranch, along a nice flowing creek, where he built a cabin and grazed his own small herd of cattle. Nevertheless, he worked very well with Elizabeth and the two soon became good friends. So much so that Elizabeth gifted him with a fine sorrel mare with four white stockings and a white star on her forehead. The mare would become his favorite saddle horse.

47

About this time, nearly 500 VD cattle were driven over Zenobia Basin. It should be noted that many writers have inaccurately attributed the notorious incident in Brown's Park where nearly 500 Middlesex Flying VD cattle were driven over a cliff in Zenobia Basin, to Elizabeth Bassett. According to Jesse S. Hoy, no friend of the Bassett family, it was Matt Rash: "Matt Rash Instructs Lou Fisher in the new way to do business...The Bassett Gang steal VD cattle."

Matthew "Matt" Madison Rash, Bassett Ranch foreman, would be the first to be murdered in Brown's Park by hired killer, Tom Horn. *Museum of Northwest Colorado*

According to Brown's Park historian, John Rolfe Burroughs, Rash was caught "red-handed" in rustling VD cattle and "rimrocked 500 VD cattle in Zenobia Basin." Hoy went on to describe Rash's involvement:

> This fracas between Lou Fisher and Bale Herndon on one side, and Matt Rash and Griff Yarnell on the other, was brought about when Fisher found the hide of a beef bearing the the Two Bar brand that had been butchered on the range and the meat hauled away in a wagon. Fisher followed the wagon tracks to Matt Rash's cabin and found

four quarters of beef which fitted the hide, but there was no one home. Later in the day, Fisher and Bale Herndon met Rash and Yarnell on the Rock Springs wagon road south of the Two Bar ranch, just across the state line in Colorado. Fisher questioned Rash about the beef and hide, told him what he found: the hide on the range and the meat at the cabin. Rash told Fisher it was none of his damned business, and not to interfere with his affairs. At the same time [he] drew his revolver and did his best to club Fisher over the head...following which Yarnell struck Herndon on the head several times with his six gun. While the fight with fists on one side, and six-shooters on the other, was in progress, Fisher, seeing the battle was going against him, told Herndon to go to the ranch and get Winchesters. Herndon started on his errand. Rash and Yarnell beat it to Yarnell's ranch.

Conversely, a local rancher, Carl Davidson, who rode many roundups with Rash as a teenager, recounted several incidents of Rash returning strays to their rightful owners.

Isom Dart, a young black man who arrived in the Park to escape a shady past, also enjoyed the kindness of his employer, Elizabeth Bassett. He too, had his own cabin away from the Bassett ranch, on Cold Spring Mountain, northwest of the Bassett ranch. While working at the Bassett ranch, Dart would often take time to interact with the Bassett children. As the children grew older they were each taught to ride horses. Dart taught the children to rope and ride. In her memoirs, Ann describes happy childhood times when the ranch hands would put on bucking contests for the children to watch. Ann later described a fond childhood memory:

Clean hay from the stack was spread on the ground. In the evening when the day's work was finished, the fun began. Each bucking cowboy on all fours, topped by his rider, came bounding out, rearing, sun fishing, and performing all the antics of a wild and vicious bronco being ridden for the first time, with the little rider hanging on for dear life, gripping

49

with his knees and holding moccasined feet tight to the flanks, one hand grasping a silk handkerchief tied in back of the broncos "front legs." This show was conducted in the regular manner; horses and riders named, an announcer appointed, and purses awarded to the best riders. Benches were placed for the spectators, and admission was charged. The top rail of the corral fence was the judge's stand. Riders stayed on until they exhausted their "bucking horses" or fell off. Roping was one of the attractions, each contestant had one throw at a human horse bucking. For this act, one or both feet had to be caught with the first throw. George Bassett, when only five years-old, was the champion roper.

George Bassett (at far right) at the Bassett summer cattle camp at Zenobia Peak on Diamond Mountain. *Museum of Northwest Colorado*

Ann explained: "Learning to ride in early childhood was a necessity. For training in balance, bucking contests were improvised. Our hay corral was the arena. From this training we developed what proved to be quite a game."

Elbert "Eb" Bassett became one of the best ropers in the area and his younger brother, George, was quite accomplished in his own right. Young Ann became quite adept with the lariat. All of this was due to Dart's kindness, patience, and skilled instruction. The lessons learned would serve Ann well in the years to come as she rode with a vengeance in her fight to keep her family's ranch.

Isom Dart worked for Elizabeth Bassett and later, Jim McKnight on Cold Spring Mountain. Dart was also murdered by Tom Horn. *Museum of Northwest Colorado*

CHAPTER NOTES AND SOURCE INFORMATION

Josie's quote regarding the birth of Anna Marie Bassett, is from her taped interviews conducted by Murl Messersmith, July 6, 1961 at Dinosaur National Monument, Jensen, Utah. A typewritten account is available at the Museum of Northwest Colorado, Craig, Colorado.

Ann Bassett Willis wrote of her life experiences in a four-part series published in the Colorado Historical Society's *Colorado Magazine*. The series, titled, "Queen Ann of Brown's Park," ran in Volume XXIX January 1952, Volume XXIX April 1952, Volume XXIX October 1952, Volume XXX January 1953. They are available at the Denver Public Library. Unless otherwise noted, the quotes attributed to Ann are from this work.

It is interesting to note that Ann's account of the Indian's help with nursing her following her birth is also found in the published excerpt of her memoir, *Scars and Two Bars*, printed in the April 1, 1943, issue of the *Moffat County Mirror*. The difference is in the spelling of the Indian names, possibly and editorial decision by the paper. I have chosen to use Ann's account from the Colorado Historical Society's *Colorado Magazine*.

The quotes of Josephine Bassett McKnight Ranney Williams Wells Morris are found in her taped interviews held at the Dinosaur National Monument, Jensen, Utah. Typewritten account available at the Museum of Northwest Colorado, Craig, Colorado.

Esther Campbell's quote regarding the Bassett mare can be found in her letters archived at the Bureau of Land Management, Vernal, Utah. An account of the event is also included on page 23 of Grace McClure's excellent work, *The Bassett Women*.

Josie claims her brother Elbert "Eb" was born in Green River, Wyoming, in 1879, during the Meeker Massacre. According to census records and family history, this is incorrect. It must be remembered that Josie was 86 years-old when she was interviewed at Dinosaur National Monument.

Ann's description of ranch work is from an excerpt of the partial memoir, *Scars and Two Bars*, published in the *Moffat County Mirror* in April 1943.

Ann's account of the first district school is from an excerpt of the partial memoir, *Scars and Two Bars*, published in the *Moffat County Mirror* in April, 1943.

Clarence Bronaugh arrived in Craig on March 12, 1891, driving a wagon team of horses. In his wagon was printing equipment and plenty of paper. The next day Bronaugh set up his printing press on the boardwalk of Yampa Avenue in Craig and published his first issue of the *Colorado Pantograph*, March 13, 1891.

Ann's remembrances of the community gatherings at her family ranch are from an excerpt of the partial memoir, *Scars and Two Bars*, published in the *Moffat County Mirror* in April 1943.

Josie Bassett uses the term "swift" in describing the Hoy's underhanded land grab. It is most likely that she meant "scrip." Scrip was buying up land for a very cheap price, once the government deemed the land had not been "proven up" or the land was not legally filed in a given time frame.

The J. S. Hoy quote is from his unpublished manuscript, *History of Brown's Park, 1917*. Courtesy, Valentine Hoy IV.

The quote regarding the Hoy brothers can be found in *An Isolated Empire: A History of Northwestern Colorado*.

The account of Jesse S. Hoy and "Mexican Joe," can be found on page 42 of Diane Kouris' *The Romantic and Notorious History of Brown's Park*.

Information regarding John Clay and the Middlesex Cattle Company comes from Athearn, *An Isolated Empire*.

The creek which flowed near Matt Rash's land is now known as Matt Creek.

The Hoy quote regarding the death of Elizabeth Bassett is in the J.S. Hoy manuscript, located at the Colorado History Center.

It should be noted that this Two Bar cattle operation was based out of Wyoming and was not Ora Haley's Colorado Two Bar cattle company.

Some believe this is Josie and Ann Bassett. Others dispute this claim. *Museum of Northwest Colorado*

THE CATTLE WAR BEGINS

Elizabeth Bassett and her hired hands soon began retaliation against the large cattle companies. The Bassett group operations consisted of rustling cattle, an all too common practice in the Park. According to historian John Rolfe Burroughs: "Technically, 'rustling cattle' was a felony offense. It is not an exaggeration to say, however, that with very few exceptions, everybody, that is everybody among the little people (nesters, settlers, homesteaders) in Brown's Park engaged in it."

With the given attitude in the Park, Elizabeth Bassett and her hired men set out rounding up loose cattle they were pretty sure belonged to the large cattle companies and then putting the Bassett brand on them. As the rustling of cattle began to achieve the desired effect, the Cattleman's Association, with financial and political power, soon spread the word that Elizabeth was the head of the Brown's Park gang of rustlers and even robbers and murderers. Elizabeth spent the next few years traveling back and forth to Hahn's Peak, fighting lawsuits. It was a long 160 mile trip by horseback or wagon for Elizabeth to appear in front of the judge of the District Court, yet she defeated every one of the lawsuits the cattle barons filed against her. In the end, Elizabeth and the ranchers of Brown's Park had achieved their goal.

Ed Rife, along with other ranchers in the area, took matters in their own hands. Faced with the threat of the Middlesex Cattle Company taking over their land, the ranchers united in force. Legally, they could not stop the Middlesex faction from moving south into Brown's Park, but they could damn sure make it difficult for their cattle to graze. Therefore, a few cattle ranchers, with Rife in the lead, went into the sheep business. Fencing the gateway to Brown's Park with their herds of sheep, the ranchers had effectively created a section of the land where there would be nothing left for the Middlesex cattle to graze upon. This marked the end of the Middlesex Cattle Company. By 1887, the ranchers had succeeded in driving out the Middlesex Cattle Company. Ann later wrote of the demise of the large cattle baron enterprise: "The Middlesex were not successful in their hope-for grab. They sold out to Ed Rife. He at once stocked the range with sheep, and small cow outfits adjoining lived in peace. This state of serenity continued for many years, or until the Haley Two Bar commenced to harass them from the east."

In 1882, a stranger by the name of Hambleton, along with two friends, came to the Bassett ranch looking for one of their hired men, Jack Rolla. Jennie Jaynes, who had been hired as cook for the ranch hands during the summer, greeted the visitors and directed the men to the barn and corrals where they could find Rolla. The strangers approached the corrals, finding Rolla with his back to them, and shot him in cold blood. Several ranch hands along with Herb and Elizabeth quickly ran to the scene and drew their guns on the strangers. Mrs. Jaynes gathered the Bassett children into the safe shelter of a nearby building. Ann later recounted the horrible murder:

> He [Jack Rolla] was a pleasant-mannered young fellow from Texas who came to the Bassett ranch in 1882. A good hand with horses, he was hired to break bronco on the ranch. It was in the late fall of that year that three strange men arrived about noon, and were asked to eat dinner with the family. While Mrs. Jaynes, who cooked for us at the time, was preparing the meal, one of the strangers asked her if Jack worked there. Mrs. Jaynes replied, "Yes, that is Jack saddling a horse at the corral." One of them pulled a gun and shot Rolla as he was reaching for a bridle. He ran behind the barn, where he fell, mortally wounded. The one who had done the shooting said his name was Hambleton and that Rolla had shot and killed his brother in Abilene, Kansas. Hambleton had trailed Jack Rolla for two years to kill him. Rolla confirmed Hambleton's statement in part,

explaining that a man of that name had married his sister. He abused the sister and Rolla had killed for it. Mother spiritedly informed Hambleton that it was not the custom of the northwest to shoot an unarmed man in the back. By the determined threat of her leveled Winchester, she lined the trio up against the bunkhouse wall, and directed the wounded Rolla to kill his assassin, or all three men, if he wanted to. Rolla was too weak to hold a gun and he died a few hours later. While mother and Mrs. Jaynes were administering to the dying cowboy, father and Perry were guarding the prisoners. Harry Hindle went to notify the settlers of the park, and to get Charles Allen, Justice of the Peace, to the scene of the crime. Night came and father began to think with deepening apprehension. A lynching could be in the making. He advised the captives to go to the barn and feed their horses, and he warned them to ride directly to the county seat, over a hundred miles away, and surrender themselves to the law. When neighbors arrived at the Bassett ranch, the murderer and his companions had escaped. Naturally, they failed to do as father had instructed, and were never heard of again. The method subscribed to by my father in the matter of advice to the shooters would have been in direct conflict with the opinion of mother and Mrs. Jaynes. Therefore, he did not commit himself and tell the true story for some time afterwards.

Ann followed up her account in her typical witty style with the statement: "The Bassett ranch had three good Winchesters... to be added to the gun rack." Later, Ann's older sister, Josie, also commented on the murder of Jack Rolla:

Our father was a very soft-hearted man and wouldn't condone a lynching, and he was also concerned about his reputation. He was postmaster, justice of the peace, and held a number of other offices. So he felt he could hardly afford to be involved in what was about to happen, and he turned the Texas cowboys loose on their word that they would turn themselves in at Hahn's Peak.

57

Josie then added this intriguing comment regarding the events following the murder of Jack Rolla:

> However, the three men rode north instead towards Rock Springs. My mother had gathered some of her boys and when they arrived back at the bunkhouse to find the men gone, they set out immediately on their trail. Somewhere near the north end of Irish Canyon they caught up to them. There was no gunfight, because the Texas boys had been disarmed at the ranch, and they were also outnumbered two or three to one. They were hanged and buried there in Irish Canyon. It was always said they left the country, but we all knew better. Jim [McKnight] told me all about it, and he should have known–he was there when it happened.

It was about this time that the Brown's Park Cemetery was established. Located on a portion of the Hoy land, the cemetery would eventually claim many Brown's Park pioneers. Ann described the event in her working memoir, *Scars and Two Bars*:

> The Brown's Park cemetery site was presented to the district by Mrs. Valentine Hoy in 1880. The first burials there were Juan Catrino, who died of pneumonia at Griff Edwards's Lodore ranch; Fred Hook, who died from tuberculosis at James Warren's ranch; and Jack Rolla, who was murdered at the Bassett ranch by men who said they were from Texas.

Ann goes on to describe how the community came together for funerals and burials:

> For burial the rough boxes were neatly lined by the women with whatever they had at hand. Louie Carro's coffin was lined with mother's white satin wedding dress. Many wedding dresses were used for that purpose. Mrs. Chas. Allen conducted the funerals, Mr. Sears offered the prayer and Tom Davenport led the singing. "Home on the Range" was a favorite in those days.

In 1889, Elizabeth's hired hands took things too far, although subsequent court testimony would reveal no proof of Elizabeth's involvement. Apparently, on November 5, 1889, Isom Dart, Jack Fitch and Angus McDougall entered the home of Henry (Harry) Hoy and stole many items. The trio then torched the house, the barn, a shed, and the haystacks. Hoy swore out a complaint at the Routt County District Court in

George Bassett as a teenager.
Museum of Northwest Colorado

Hahn's Peak. The charge was grand larceny and arson against Dart, Fitch and McDougall. Hoy's brother, Adea, also filed a complaint against Dart and McDougall, charging them with altering the brands on three of his horses.

Court convened at Hahn's Peak on January 21, 1890. The three accused men appeared before the judge to hear the charges. Bail was set at 600 dollars for each man. Several small Brown's Park ranchers raised the money for the bail, including J. C. Allen, C. W. Barrington, George Law, and Mrs. Elizabeth Bassett. With bond posted, the three men walked out of court with the promise they would appear for their trial date set for September. When court convened on September 9, 1890, Fitch and McDougall

Herbert "Eb" Bassett Jr. *Museum of Northwest Colorado*

were in attendance. However, Isom Dart did not appear and it would be quite some time before he reappeared in Brown's Park.

Prosecuting witnesses for the Hoys were William Ames, Perry Carmichael, Julia Hoy, Valentine S. Hoy, and John Martin. Among witnesses for the defense were Elizabeth Bassett, her son, Sam Bassett, and Thomas Davenport. Jack Fitch was found guilty of arson and sentenced to five years in the Colorado State Penitentiary at Canon City. Angus McDougall was also found guilty of arson and altering brands on the Hoy horses. He was sentenced to seven years of hard labor at the Colorado State Penitentiary.

For a time, the Bassett family continued with their routine daily life.

On December 11, 1892, just as the Christmas season was being celebrated in the Bassett household, tragedy occurred in the family. The ambitious and always energetic Elizabeth suddenly fell ill and took to her bed. Early the previous morning, she arose from bed when she heard a ruckus outside her window. Running from the cabin to investigate, she saw that her favorite milk cow was caught up in a herd of cattle being rounded up by the large cattle barons. Furious, Elizabeth saddled her horse and rode out to claim her cow. With a few choice words, she cut her cow out of the herd and returned it to the Bassett ranch. It proved to be a trying day for Elizabeth and she retired to bed early that night.

Mary Eliza Chamberlain Miller Bassett died the following day, at the age of 37. She was the first to be buried in the private cemetery on the Bassett ranch. Elizabeth's older daughter, Josie, later recalled the sad event:

> She went to bed at night all right, and woke up about four o'clock in the morning just deathly sick. Just terribly sick. Father was there and Jim McKnight was there, and—I don't know—some of the cowboys. And they couldn't get a doctor, of course. All they could do—all they thought of was hot applications and that relieved her, of course, but she died.

The *Empire Courier* newspaper in Craig, Colorado, reported the death of Elizabeth Bassett as a news story, rather than an obituary. The article appeared in the December 16, 1892, issue of the paper:

A Sad Event

A messenger from Brown's Park arrived Monday bringing the sad intelligence of the death of Mrs. E. Bassett. Her children, Sam, Josie and Anna who have been attending school, immediately started for home, accompanied by Mrs. William Morgan. Mrs. Bassett's death occurred on Sunday after an illness of two weeks. The deceased is one of the best known women in the county, where she has lived since the earliest settlement. She was a natural pioneer possessing the most remarkable courage and energy. She was highly esteemed by those who best knew her and commanded the respect of those who from conflicting business interests were her enemies. The most conspicuous and admirable trait in Mrs. Bassett's character was her unwavering loyalty and devotion to her friends. She was only 35 years of age and apparently in the meridian of health and vigor. The sympathy of the community is extended to the motherless children.

There are a few errors in this article. At the time of her death, Mary Eliza Chamberlain Miller Bassett, born in 1855, was 37 years-old, not 35. Also, Elizabeth had not been ill for two weeks. Josie later recalled: "I was away at St. Mary's when my mother died. I didn't go back, I stayed home then because my father needed me so bad. My father was perfectly lost. I had been two years at St. Mary's to November, two years and a half, pert near."

Josie always believed her mother died of appendicitis, while Ann believed her mother's death was from a miscarriage. The Bassett family grief was deep. The matriarch of the family and anchor, particularly for Josie and Ann, was gone.

The only neighbor in the Park to "damn her" according to writer, Grace McClure, was Jesse S. Hoy. Having had several conflicts with Elizabeth, and others, Hoy eventually stopped his attempt to overtake the small ranchers in Brown's Park. After her death, J. S. Hoy was quoted as saying: "We came into Brown's Park to run the nesters out. We started it, but Elizabeth Bassett finished it, and she finished it good!"

Perhaps. However, while it is not known which of the cattle baron companies was responsible for attempting to steal Elizabeth's favorite milk cow, in the end, the act resulted in the early demise of the "natural pioneer possessing the most remarkable courage and energy," as the *Empire Courier* aptly characterized Elizabeth Bassett. While it was Elizabeth Bassett who began the war against the large cattle companies, it would be her daughter, Ann, who would carry on her legacy and finally finish it. Her sister, Josephine, would later say: "Ann was a visionary and up in the air a good part of the time."

Herbert "Herb" Bassett, (seated) the patriarch of the family. *Museum of Northwest Colorado*

This Memory Card was handed out at the funeral of Mary Eliza Chamberlain Miller Bassett in December 1892. *Museum of Northwest Colorado*

CHAPTER NOTES AND SOURCE INFORMATION

The quote of John Rolfe Burroughs regarding cattle rustling can be found on page 56 of *Where the Old West Stayed Young.*

Ann's quote regarding the Middlesex Cattle Company is contained in her published account, "Queen Ann of Brown's Park." *Colorado Magazine*, Denver Public Library, Volume XXIX January 1952.

The account of Jack Rolla's murder can be found in Ann Bassett Willis' unpublished memoirs of Ann Bassett Willis, held at the Denver Public Library, Western History Collection.

Josie's version of Rolla's murder comes from her taped interviews, held at the Dinosaur National Monument, Jensen, Utah. Typewritten account is available at the Museum of Northwest Colorado, Craig, Colorado.

Details of the establishment of the Brown's Park Cemetery can be found in Wommack, *From the Grave.*

Information concerning the outcome of Henry (Harry) Hoy's lawsuit against Elizabeth Bassett and a few of her hired hands comes from the District Court records, Ninth Judicial District, Colorado, 1890.

Members of the Bassett family buried in the cemetery on the family ranch can be found in Wommack, *From the Grave.*

Mary Eliza Chamberlain Miller Bassett was born on August 25, 1855.

Josie's account of her mother's death is from her taped interviews at the Dinosaur National Monument, Jensen, Utah. Typewritten account is available at the Museum of Northwest Colorado, Craig, Colorado.

The J. S. Hoy quote can be found in Burroughs, *Where the Old West Stayed Young.*

Charlie Crouse ranch. *Museum of Northwest Colorado*

THE OUTLAW ELELMENT

The Bassett ranch had long been known as a welcoming place to neighbors and even strangers, with no questions asked. Herb and Elizabeth Bassett may or may not have known of the outlaw element that frequented the area. Nevertheless, the Bassett children were raised in the open atmosphere of the West. Hiram "Hi" Bernard, who would later marry Ann Bassett, recalled: "The old Bassett Ranch has some time or another housed most everyone in this Park or part of the North West. Charley Sparks made his home there, when he first came west as a boy, from North Carolina. Sparks is a wealthy man now."

Both Ann and her older sister, Josie, loved their childhood years in Brown's Park. The attractive Bassett girls were well-skilled with horses, and roping, and could shoot nearly as well as any of the hired hands on the Bassett ranch. The Bassett girls, as sisters often do, had their share of conflict with each other. As the oldest Bassett daughter, Josie was expected to look out for her younger siblings. Ann resented the constant scoldings from her older sister and often went to her parents in tears. Of course, Josie would be scolded, to the delight of Ann.

Ann inherited her mother's wild temper. During the range war between her mother and the Hoys, Ann would throw rocks at any of the Hoys who happened to pass by the school yard. Following their elementary schooling, Herb sent each of his children to Craig to finish their education.

In the spring of 1886, twelve year-old Josie and her eight year-old sister Ann, attended one of Charlie Crouse's local horse races. Crouse was known throughout the Park for his prized horses as well as his occasional cattle rustling. Outlaw and part-time

Brown's Park resident near Diamond Mountain, Matt Warner, whose real name was Willard Erastus Christiansen, later wrote: "...Charley Crause, that good-hearted old cattle rustler from Brown's Park..."

One of Crouse's hired hands, exceptional with horses, was a man known as George Cassidy (George Leroy Parker) This particular horse race was greatly attended as Crouse's sorrel gelding was to race against Ken Hatch's award-winning black mare from Ashley Valley. George Cassidy rode Crouse's sorrel thoroughbred gelding to a roaring finish. Ann later wrote: "We were proud of that horse. He could not only run but he was a beautiful animal. The young rider was George Cassidy and later became known as Butch Cassidy, the outlaw."

So caught up in the moment, both Bassett girls became enamored with the handsome blond man who won the horse race. The girls found any and every excuse they could to visit the Crouse ranch just to be near the dashing cowboy. While this became great entertainment during the hot summer of 1886, their efforts often gained them no more than a smile or nod from Cassidy. As summer turned to fall, both girls were back in school and their summer crush was soon a fading memory. According to Ann: "Cassidy continued to work for Charlie Crouse for a year then went away. That is what I personally know of the notorious Butch Cassidy–whose exploits are a favorite topic of all the old liars, young liars and damn liars in the northwest..."

However, true to the sibling rivalry, Josie had a different version:

> I thought he was the most dashing and handsome man I had ever seen. I was such a young thing, and giddy as most teenagers are, and I looked upon Butch as my knight in shining armor. But he was more interested in his horse than he was in me, and I remember being very put out by that. I went home after being snubbed by him and stamped my foot on the floor in frustration.

Robert Leroy "Butch" Cassidy possibly during his time in Brown's Park.
Denver Public Library

Cassidy would leave the area for months on end but would eventually wander back to Brown's Park. Surrounded by mountains, not to mention close to three state borders, with plenty of water and good grazing in the valley below, Brown's Park seemed a perfect place for a hideout, and Cassidy took advantage. Forming his gang of outlaws, later the notorious Wild Bunch, Cassidy's first hideout became the area around Brown's Park. Among the various outlaws who visited, passed through, or made their home in Brown's Park, were Cassidy's close friends Matt Warner and Tom McCarty, as well as Elza Lay, George "Flat Nose" Curry, and Harry "The Sundance Kid" Longabaugh. Of Matt Warner, Josie later said: "Old Matt Warner that [Charles] Kelly writes about, why he was nothing. I'm not proud of the fact that I knew him."

Despite Ann's later claims of knowing nothing of the "notorious Butch Cassidy," the Bassetts welcomed the outlaws. They provided shelter, offered temporary work, and conducted business with them by supplying the men with beef and fresh horses. In fact, in her memoir, *Scars and Two Bars*, Ann evidently did

Elza Lay. *Denver Public Library*

Tom McCarty. *Denver Public Library*

see more of Butch Cassidy, for she wrote: "I never saw Butch Cassidy dance or get drunk, or carry a gun in sight. I am not presuming to say he was not an outlaw later. But what I do say is I had seen him many times before and after he was called an outlaw and he was at all times a well mannered fellow."

As Ann was prone to exaggeration, it does not seem to be the case in this instance. There is historic evidence that Cassidy did stay at the Bassett ranch and Ann herself later describes an event where Cassidy was present. And there is also her sister Josie's account of Cassidy at the ranch. Perhaps Ann was offering cover for her outlaw friend. Josie evidently didn't mind the added company of the outlaws at all. For she later said: "And let me say they had some cute boys with their outfit. It was a thrill to see Henry Rhudenbaugh tall, blond & handsome."

It should be noted that Josie Bassett was also prone to exaggeration, even more so than her younger sister, Ann. A case in point of out-right embellishment is this quote of Josie's. There is no evidence that Harry Longabough, alias the Sundance Kid, was in Brown's Park at this time. During the summer, Cassidy spent a great deal of time around the Bassett Ranch. He enjoyed the company of Herb Bassett, who shared his newspapers and books. But Josie, years later, had a different recollection of the twenty year-old Cassidy, describing him as, "a big dumb kid who liked to joke." Even so, it was only a matter of time before Josie and "Butch" Cassidy became lovers, according to Josie. She later recounted the teen affair of the heart: "After one of Butch's rich uncles died [euphemism for

Butch Cassidy shortly after his release prison.
Denver Public Library

a bank or train robbery,] we put him up, hiding him in the hay loft. He used to say, 'Josie, I'm lonely up here. Come out and keep me company...' He asked me... What am I going to do to keep from being bored?' Well, all I can say is, I didn't let him get bored..."

The teenage affair ended when Cassidy again left the Park and Josie was sent to Craig to finish her high school education. In 1890, at the age of sixteen, Josie's parents sent her to the Catholic finishing school, St. Mary's of the Wasatch, in Salt Lake City, Utah. This is where Josie was when she received the news of her mother's death, December 12, 1892.

(John Jarvie) 'Tis happy I am to welcome you here to our valley at
this Thanksgiving season. Not often have we been honored by so many guests.
If you will please find places at the tables I will tell you a bit about us,
and the hole, and why we are gathered here today.

My name is John Jarvie, born and bred in Scotland. Aye, and away from the
bonnie land these many years. So I dnow you'll grant me the privelege of
using my notes, time dulls an old man's memory. By now, most of you know I
have the stage-coach stop, as some of you gave just crossed the ferry. Also
I have the stone office in the Hole- set up in 1869, it was. Also I presume
you know that the stage line runs from Ft. Duchesne, Utah to Rock Springs
and Green River City, Wyo. Both ways - every day! Indeed, we're proud of
the record- for 'tis a long, hard journey.

Look about you and you will note the extent of this broad valley, surrounded
on three sides by rugged mountains, and cut by the deep Green River. Brown's
Hole it was called first, by Bible-back Brown, a French fur trapper. A fine
place, he thought, to hole up for the winter. Later, it became Brown's Park,
a haven to people from all walks of life. Some have selected choice spots to
call home. Others, to rest awhile before drifting on to personal pursuits.
Of this last are our hosts at dinner today- the Wild Bunch- and the Bender
Gang.

Aye, and they have spared nothing to prove that they remember and appreciate
the niceties of a home with fine food and cultural entertainment. I am proud
to introduce- Butch Cassidy
                    Elza Lay
                    Isam Dart
                    Billie Bender
                    Lea Megs
Before they serve us this bountiful meal- a brief prayer of Thanksgiving.
"Dear Heavenly Father, we thank Thee for Thy goodness and mercy, and pray
Thee to bless this food of which we are about to partake, that it may nourish
our souls with the strenght and endurance to follow Thee and to continue to
live in peace here in our valley. Amen.

Nationalities Represented

John Jarvie	Scotland
The Davenports and Walter Scrivoner *scrivners*	England
Lu Warren	Ireland
Jimmie Greenson	Australia
John Erickson & other Scandanavians	Sweden
John Dempshire	Yugoslavia
Harry Hendle	Wales
Mary & Joe Mestas-(newlyweds)	Mexican & Indian
Leanor Strickland	Canada
Solomon Rouff	Germany
Martin Gofanti	

Hosts were all Americans
Cook- (Dart)- Negro (American)

All were directly from these countries- not descendents.

A portion of Esther Campbell's 1953 program titled "Thanksgiving 1895."
Uintah County Libary, Vernal, Utah

This was a particularly difficult time in Josie's life. Not only
was she grieving for the loss of her mother, she also came to the
realization that she was pregnant with Jim McKnight's child. On
March 21, 1893, 19 year-old Josephine Bassett and James Fielding
McKnight were married in Green River City, Utah. Their son
Crawford would be born in Brown's Park on July 12, 1893.

Following her mother's death, Ann completed her local education in Craig. Herb then sent Ann to St. Mary's of the Wasatch for the Spring 1893 term. This was the same school where her older sister had received high marks in all subjects. While Josie enjoyed her experience at the school, Ann hated it. At the end of the first term, the nuns asked Ann's father to find another school for his daughter. Josie later recalled: "Oh she [Ann] went one year at St. Mary's, but she didn't like it. And I liked it and I'd liked to have gone back, I thought it was wonderful, and it is wonderful. It is the most wonderful place I ever knew of for girls, yes it 'tis. I always liked it and I have been back a lot of times just to visit."

Ann wrote in her memoirs, that she attended "Miss" Potter's School for Girls in Boston, Massachusetts. Josie later told her family that "this was just another of Ann's exaggerations." It is difficult to know the truth, as Ann was prone to "exaggerations" as her sister stated, but it must also be remembered that Ann and Josie had a long history of sibling rivalry.

However, Mrs. Potter's School for Girls located in Everett, a suburb of Boston, advertised in several local and national publications, such as the Critic, which ran several ads in their 1894 issues, the time period Ann says she attended the school. The fact remains that Ann was indeed away from Brown's Park attending "a" school

Anna Marie Bassett about the time she returned home following her schooling in 1895.
Denver Public Library

in the East from 1893 to 1895. In any case, Ann wrote of her experience in leaving Brown's Park for the school:

> Then came a more drastic change in my life– I was sent to the select "Miss Potter's School for Girls" in the exclusive suburbs of Boston. I departed from home with confidence, anticipating a further enjoyable experience. I found myself in a place so strange it might as well have been located in a foreign land. Not, only strange, but at times unbearably disagreeable. Endless months dragged past in a restricted social atmosphere of quaint gentility and, baked beans. My imagination could never have pictured such a situation. I was stifled. My inner turbulence lacked even the relief of proper exercise.

Ann went on to describe one of the many experiences at this school:

> The school employed a riding 'Mawstah' to teach the girls correct positions in the saddle and how to post. One morning about a dozen of us were lined up for inspection before taking off for a decorous canter over chosen bridle paths. Everything appeared ship-shape. But there was rebellion in my soul, revolt that demanded action. The "Mawstah" walked back a few yards for some words with one of the stable boys, That was my Heaven-given chance to air 'rink' dun out a little. I was perched like a monkey on a stick, atop of a locked old saline gelding with one glass eye. I threw my right leg up over the side saddle and raked his flanks. Then uttering a wild yell that must have scared him half to death, I put him through several range stunts while the girls screamed with glee. The outraged "Mawstah" came on the run giving off a stream of sarcasm meant for me. He grabbed for my bridle reins as the same time ordering me sharply to "dismount." He got nowhere reaching for my bridle. I was completely riled up by that time. I swung the horse about, with a prancing and rearing

he had probably never before even attempted. Leaning from my saddle, I exclaimed vehemently, "Go to hell, you repulsive, little monkey-faced skunk!" His eyes nearly popped from his head with shock, he turned and ran for the school office to report the scandalous event. Our riding lesson was promptly canceled for that day. And I was brought before the stoney-faced faculty, on the carpet, with all the girls of my riding class also there to testify to my use of profane language. Not one of them could remember a word I had said! Indeed, they had not heard anything out of the ordinary.

Despite her displays of mischievous behavior, Ann did well in school. She gained a sense of eastern refinement and style. Ann later reflected on her time in both schools writing:

About a year after Mother passed away I began to be a problem to my father. Although wise in many ways, [father] was too tender and kind-hearted to control a girl of my temperament. I was about as responsive to [his] gentle rule of love as granite on a winter morning...Not until twenty years later did I realize that I was then being disciplined and educated for the finer things in life.

With her schooling complete, Ann longed to return to her western home in Brown's Park. She later said the experience left "a deep impression." When she finally did return in late 1895, she brought with her all the latest fashions in clothing and even a new look: Ann was wearing makeup. Ann was a very attractive woman. According to John Rolfe Boroughs, Brown's Park early historian:

Arriving at maturity, she stood five feet three inches tall, weighed a hundred and fifteen pounds, possessed an 'hour glass' figure without the assistance of corsets, which loathing them, she seldom wore, and had large, deceptively mild gray eyes and naturally wavy auburn hair. As spirited as she was high-strung, and highly intelligent, suiting her own convenience or caprice Ann could play the role of cultured young gentlewoman full to over-flowing with gentility plus the innate Bassett charm; or she could be perfect little hell-cat capable of throwing and breaking things, in command of a vocabulary that would cause a livery-stable hanger-on to blush for shame.

When Ann returned home, she wasted no time in letting everyone know she was back. She hosted many community get-togethers and visited regularly with the women of Brown's Park. Following the death of her mother, Ann, now a young woman, took over the family ranch with one goal: to protect her family's interest and maintain the ranch. Known for her iron-willed attitude, Ann was headstrong and quite demanding. She was not arrogant or superior. Quite the contrary. She got along very well with the hired hands. She rolled her own cigarettes from a pouch of Bull Durham tobacco, in the days when women didn't smoke, and drank her whiskey straight. Older sister Josie strongly disapproved of Ann's unconventional behavior. It only made Ann more obstinate. Ann later commented on her behavior:

> Through trial and error I became a specialist at evading mother's staff of authority. With the speed of a wapiti I would race to the bunkhouse, that place of many attractions, where saddle-galled cow punchers congregated to sing range ballads and squeak out doleful tunes on the fiddle. Somewhere in a secluded corner an absorbing round of poker was sure to be in session.

One of the occasional hired hands was a charming young man who had drifted west from Boston, Massachusetts, by the name of William Ellsworth "Elza" Lay. He and Ann formed a close friendship that would last for years. In fact, throughout the many events of Lay's life, he remained close to the entire Bassett family, sending several letters to both Ann and her older brother, Sam. Ann describes the first time she met Lay:

Members of a Brown's Park posse. Included in this group is Isom Dart, fourth from right. *Museum of Northwest Colorado*

When haying time drew near, the summer of 1894, father sent a wagon to Rock Springs for hands. With the crew of haymakers that came to the ranch was Elza Lay, a well bred appearing young fellow with a winning smile and perfect manners. He was a capable workman, strong and active, with a gentle good nature that won the hearts of old and young alike. Elza remained on the ranch for a year...When the year was up he went back to Rock Springs. Not long afterward rumors circulated that he had joined forces with Butch Cassidy, and that they were carrying on a series of bank and train robberies.

Ann hosted the 1896 Thanksgiving dinner party for all the families in Brown's Park. The event was held at the Davenport ranch. From her memoirs, Ann says that among the local families such as the Jarvies and Davenports, guests included Matt Rash, Isom Dart, Elza Lay, Butch Cassidy, and "Harry Roudenbaugh." In Ann's writings published in the *Colorado Magazine*, she described in great detail, what the women wore.

Esther Davenport had the pretty dress for the party. A yellow silk mull over yellow taffeta, she looked very pretty. Now I will tell you what I wore at the party–silk mull powder blue accordion pleated from top to bottom, camesole and petticoat of taffeta, peter pan collar, buttoned in the back, puffed sleeves to the elbows. The mull pleated well and how it swished over the taffeta undies. For the stocking–lace made of silk and lisle thread black to match shoes. They were precious and worn only for parties. They cost $3.00 a pair and lasted a long time. I wore my hair in three curles fastened at nap of neck held in place by large barrett beau catcher curl on forehead. Spring heeled shoes like the babydoll shoes shown in the catalogues now.

Of her sister Josie's dress, Ann recalled, in kind words, given their sibling rivalry: "Josie's dress for the party was a sage green wool. Many–gored skirt, tight to the knees then flared to the floor to sweep up the dirt. Josie was married, I was not. By the way, Josie played a 'Zither' and rather well. She was accompanied by Sam Bassett on the fiddle and Joe Davenport with a guitar."

It is interesting to note that Ann's friend, Esther Campbell wrote a program reenacting the "Outlaw Thanksgiving," in 1953. Campbell along with other members of her history group reenacted the event in November 1953. In attendance was none other than Josie Bassett Morris, who was present at the original event. The program, dated November 14, 1953, contained information Campbell received from both Ann and Josie. However, Esther Campbell placed the date of the event in 1895 instead of 1896. Nowhere in any of Ann or Josie's writings for that matter, is the date listed as 1895. Nor could it have been, for Butch Cassidy was not released from prison until January of the following year.

Cassidy returned to the Park in 1896. He was released early, January 19, 1896, from a two-year stay in the Wyoming State Penitentiary for horse theft. Cassidy reunited with his friend Matt Warner, at Diamond Mountain. During his many sojourns away from the Park, he had spent time working at various ranches across the Colorado state line, including the Two Bar Cattle Company, then headquartered near Casper. He spent at least one winter in Rock Springs, Wyoming, where he worked as a butcher in a local meat store. Many historians claim this is where Robert Leroy Parker, alias George Cassidy, acquired the nickname "Butch." However, Matt Warner states in one of his many yarns, that he and Tom McCarty gave him the nickname after a shooting incident during their trip to Brown's Park. Warner had a shotgun that "kicked so hard when we fired it, it nearly took us apart and we called it 'Butch.'" The two men goaded Cassidy into shooting the gun. When he shot the gun, Warner relates, "It knocked him flat on his back in the mud and water alongside of that rock. He flopped and floundered like a fish and by the time he was out, he was smeared with mud from his head to his feet. Tom and me nearly fell of our horses laughing. We named him Butch after that kicking needle gun."

The outlaws such as Cassidy, Warner, McCarty, Lay, Harry "the Sundance Kid" Longabaugh, and Harvey "Kid Curry" Logan, often hid out in the area following their first bank robbery back in 1889. Cassidy, Warner, and McCarty had lit out for Brown's Park following their robbery of the San Miguel Bank in Telluride, Colorado, on June 24, 1889. A few days later the three men arrived at Charlie Crouse's ranch. He provided fresh horses for the men and led them to a well-hidden cabin on his property, south of the Green River. Crouse's land was located approximately three miles west of the Colorado state line in Utah, a nearly inaccessible rocky location in the Uintah Mountains, and a few miles southwest of the Wyoming border.

Jesse S. Hoy despised the outlaw element seeping into Brown's Park, with good reason as it would turn out. Hoy later wrote:

> They were acquainted with the area and made their way to that rendezvous for all the bad men of the country at that time, Browns Park, in northwestern Routt county, which was infested by the Powder Springs gang and was a regular stopping place for an organized band of crooks and murders as they plied their nefarious trade through

Montana, Wyoming, Colorado, Utah and New Mexico. Butch Cassidays wild riders, the Hole-in-the-Wall gang and all the other outlaws that went on the trail have at some time or another stopped temporarily in Browns Park. The region lent itself well to the purpose of men hiding from the law. It is a large, mountainous sparcely settled, cedar covered region in which it is easy to evade pursuit.

It was a fabulous strategic location, as lawmen could rarely track the outlaws and the close proximity to the three border states made it difficult for law enforcement to judge jurisdiction. The area soon became known as the "Outlaw Trail." It was one of the three major hideouts used along the trail stretching from the Hole-in-the-Wall area in Johnson County, Wyoming, and Robbers' Roost, an isolated desert area along the lower Green River in southern Utah.

When Cassidy was in Brown's Park, he divided his time between the hidden cabin and the Bassett ranch where he worked for Herb Bassett and spent hours in his library. Ann Bassett later explained the situation: "There was a reason why the people of Brown's Park were not interested in starting a row with the outlaws. In the first place, we did not know what their business really was. And we were pretty good at tending to our own affairs. They started no trouble with us and we let them alone. The young people of each group mingled and liked each other."

Supporting Ann's claim, James Carl Sizer, a former range foreman for Ora Haley's Two Bar ranch, later recounted that:

> You continually encountered a string of 'strangers'
> drifting through the country. If they had no camp outfit,
> they stopped at some ranch, or drifted from one ranch to
> another by easy stages. If a rancher did not treat them
> right, he might find their worn-out horses on the range
> after they left, and never find his own. Since the ranchmen
> could not afford to lose their saddle horses, they kept open
> house for all comers, asked no questions, and treated all
> alike as a matter of self protection. It was this situation
> that gave Brown's Park a hard name, and caused some of

the settlers in there to be accused of harboring a bunch of outlaws, when in fact they were not.

Cassidy became popular within the community, dividing his time between friendly horse races and the hospitality of the Bassett ranch. He and his companions felt safe in the region due to the community support and the fact that few law officers dared venture across the many treacherous trails into the isolated area. It was here, in this remote and rugged land, that Butch Cassidy formed his outlaw gang known as "The Wild Bunch." The outlaws who hid out in this unusual area of state territories knew the geography well. They easily managed to elude their pursuers. Various members of the Wild Bunch would return to the safety of the Park following their outlaw deeds.

Butch Cassidy was held in high regard by the Bassetts and most of the inhabitants of Brown's Park. He was friendly to all he met and was known for his sense of humor. The good-natured and fun-loving Cassidy became a regular at the barn dances. Ann later wrote of her limited association with the outlaws, particularly, her friendship with Elza Lay, an original member of Cassidy's Wild Bunch: "He was a likable Englishman...we did not pry into his affairs, we had accepted Elza Lay as our friend, and friendship among our community was no light bond. We were in a constant struggle to protect our land and our interests on the range where our living was at stake. Bank robbers were not a menace to personal interests, and we had no reason to fear them."

Ann even arranged several romantic meetings for her friend Lay, and Matilda Maud Davis of Ashley Valley, Utah. Ann recounted their first meeting:

> A crowd of young people arrived from Utah to put up hay on the Hoy meadows simultaneously with one of Elza's secret visits. We at once planned a dance with him as special guest. There Elza was introduced to a beautiful brunette, a girl of irreproachable background. She was the belle of the evening and rightfully so. They were spontaneously drawn to each other, and were a pair mighty good to look at.

81

When the two agreed to marry, it was Ann who arranged for a local minister to perform the ceremony at a site overlooking the Green River. Ann described the event: "On a lonely mountainside, Mabel and Elza were solemnly married by that daring clergyman. Immediately after the ceremony was performed, I got on my horse and rode for home."

It is unclear why Ann referred to Maud Davis as "Mabel." Perhaps it was a nickname or the fading memory of the 74 year-old Ann Bassett Willis at the time of this particular writing. Ann went on in her writings to say: "Elza and Butch returned to Brown's Park at times, but we did not pry into affairs concerning their private lives, for we were not the instigators of the short cut to riches Elza was taking and we did not channel the course he had set."

Ann's open kindness toward the outlaw element caused rumor and suspicion. Among the many rumors, she denied the most controversial: that she headed the Bassett Gang of outlaws and that she was a cattle rustler. The first denial was true, the Bassett Gang, if it existed at all, was rumored of nearly 20 years previously, when Ann's mother, Elizabeth, was alive and Ann was a young girl. The second denial, however, was highly questionable, as Ann would soon enter into a range war the likes of which her mother never would have imagined.

In February 1898, two tragic events occurred in Brown's Park, and the Bassett ranch specifically, that would be the beginning of the end for the outlaw element in the Park. J. S. Hoy had filed complaints of cattle rustling and murder against John Jack "Judge" Bennett and Patrick Louis "P. L." Johnson.

At the time, Johnson, rumored to have killed a man, was leasing a portion of Hoy's land and Hoy suspected he was the reason a few of his cattle were missing. Bennett had an interesting outlaw background. He possessed a long criminal record culminating with a charge of "assault with attempt to commit murder," following a December 28, 1887, incident in Lander, Wyoming. Convicted of the charge, he spent five years in the Wyoming State prison in Laramie. Released on April 26, 1892, he roamed the area of Brown's Park, becoming a familiar figure. Jesse S. Hoy would later write:

Bennett was a gun man, and a cattle thief. He was one of the men for whom the sheriff had a warrant and which had occasioned his trip to Browns Park. He was a member of the Powder Springs gang of outlaws.

Bennett was so handy with a gun that he thought no man or set of men dared to attempt to arrest him, and he had threaten to kill nearly every man in the valley. One man he had disliked in particular, and said he intended to "shoot off an arm and a leg to see how he could move around."

Josie Bassett McKnight later said: "Johnson was a fool. He got in with Bennett, and Bennett used the Valentine Hoy place as a hang-out."

The Hoy complaint alleged that on February 17, 1898, at the ranch of Valentine Hoy near Pine Mountain along Red Creek, just over the state line in Wyoming, P. L. Johnson had shot and killed 16 year-old Willie Strang. It was an innocent action by the young boy that brought the ire of Johnson and the death of Strang. Strang had spilled water on Johnson's shirt, either accidentally or playfully. Johnson's reaction startled Strang and he ran away from the scene. Johnson followed him to the barn, raised his pistol and fired. The bullet hit the young boy in the back, and Willie Strang lingered in agony before his death several hours later.

Johnson, along with Bennett, immediately left the Hoy ranch, on a pair of Hoy horses, heading south for Powder Springs northeast of Brown's Park, on the state line of Colorado and Wyoming. Forty-six year-old Charlie Crouse formed a posse and tracked the men as far as they could. Meanwhile, Valentine Hoy and William Pidgeon, a witness to the shooting of young Strang, buried the boy on the Hoy land.

Thirty-six year-old Routt County Sheriff Charles Willis Neiman, received the warrants a week later and left Steamboat Springs, near the county seat of Hahn's Peak, on February 25th, with the warrants in hand. He knew Hoy's ranch was just over the state line in Wyoming, but had no idea that the outlaws had gone to Powder Springs. He had surmised that the cattle in the alleged

David Lant (left) and Harry Tracy. *Museum of Northwest Colorado*

rustling charge may have been taken to the Colorado portion of Brown's Park. This had always been a difficult situation for the sheriff's department regarding jurisdiction, and the very reason outlaws chose Brown's Park as a hideout. J. S. Hoy later remarked on the character of Sheriff Neiman:

> Charles W. Neiman, now a cattleman, [was] as brave a man and as competent an officer as ever served the people of this county, was elected sheriff in 1895 and re-elected in 1897 [and again in 1902 and 1909].
>
> He had for years been a cowboy and was familiar with every hill and gulch in the county, he had put in many years riding the ranges of Snake River and the lower country, having been stationed in Brown's Park for three years, looking after cattle.
>
> In February, 1898, Sheriff Neiman was notified that a justice of the peace in Brown's Park [J.S. Hoy] had issued a warrant for Johnstone and Bennett accused of killing cattle on the ranges and disposing of the meat.

Meanwhile, at Powder Springs, Bennett and Johnson met up with two dangerous escaped convicts, David Lant from the Utah State Penitentiary, and Harry Tracy, who had murdered three guards, from the Oregon State Penitentiary. The new group formed a plan. Bennett would stay behind, purchasing supplies, and would join the other three at Lodore Canyon, the eastern edge of Brown's Park.

Sheriff Neiman arrived in Craig, where he enlisted the assistance of Routt County deputy sheriff Ethan Allen Farnham. The men spent the night at the Vaughn ranch and left the following morning for Brown's Park and the Bassett ranch where they hoped to obtain information and raise a posse. J. S. Hoy described the route the posse faced:

> It is forty miles from the Vaughn ranch to A.H. Bassetts ranch, which was to be headquarters on the expedition. The road surmounts the divide between Bear and snake rivers, crosses the latter river at the Two Bar ranch, thence over a divide, and down a long gulch known as Boone draw, to the Vermillion, which flows into Green River. The road is sandy, and traveling dificult much of the way. When going down this draw, the officers occasionally could catch glimpses of moving objects far ahead of them and they quickened their speed in order to get a closer inspection.

Along the way they observed a group of horse riders. As Neiman attempted to approach them, the group fled. Arriving that evening at the Bassett ranch, they were greeted by 63 year-old Herb Bassett, two of his sons, 13 year-old George, 17 year-old Elbert "Eb" and 20 year-old John Strang, the older brother of the murdered Willie Strang.

Following supper, Sheriff Neiman persuaded John Strang to ride out in the cover of darkness to recruit a posse. His intention was to ride off in the morning in pursuit of the men he had seen that day, as he had reason to believe they were the men he held warrants for. Shortly after midnight, Strang returned with a group of men including, Valentine Hoy, William Pidgeon, Elijah B.

Valentine Hoy. *Museum of Northwest Colorado*

Sheriff Charles Willis Neiman led the posse to capture outlaws Lant and Tracy. *Museum of Northwest Colorado*

86

"Longhorn" Thompson, Boyd Vaughn and 29 year-old Jim McKnight.

The following morning, Monday, February 28, these four men along with John Strang and Eb Bassett, left the Bassett ranch with the sheriff and his deputy. They found the trail near where Sheriff Neiman had seen the men the previous day and followed it south nearly all day. At the base of Douglas Mountain, the men discovered an abandoned campsite with camp gear, bedding, and five horses remaining at the site. Obviously aware they were being followed, they left on foot for the rugged rocky terrain of Douglas Mountain. The sheriff and his men knew it would be an ambush if they were to follow them over the rocks with no trail to follow. Therefore Sheriff Neiman made the decision to wait them out. His theory was seeing that they had no horses, the fugitives couldn't go far and with no bedding they would either come out of the rocky hills eventually or freeze to death in the cold February nights.

The next morning, March 1, 1898, a group of the posse discovered fresh footprints in the snow leading to Lodore Canyon. The posse split up. Thompson and Strang stayed at the campsite with the posse's horses, while young Bassett and Vaughn were sent to a prominent rock point where they had a commanding view of the valley below, watching in the event that the outlaws might double back. Neiman, Farnham, Hoy, Pidgeon, and McKnight then set off on foot up the side of Douglas Mountain. About mid-afternoon Neiman knew his decision was the correct one as the posse found a smoldering fire.

The posse tracking Lant and Tracy covered rock cliffs and ledges such as this.
Museum of Northwest Colorado

As Neiman was standing near the fire, Valentine Hoy started up the rocks toward a split rock. Neiman told Hoy not to get to far ahead of the posse. At that instant, two rifle shots rang out in the rock canyon, and Valentine Hoy fell, half sitting and half kneeling against the rocks. Jim McKnight was following Hoy up the rock cliff and saw one of the outlaws, later recognized as Harry Tracy. McKnight jumped out from behind a rock and attempted to grab Hoy's Winchester rifle. McKnight fired a shot toward the outlaw who immediately ducked back. For over an hour the posse hid in cover of rocks and cedar, as the outlaws above had the advantage. As for the outlaws, the only escape they had was the rushing cold waters of the Green River. As evening approached, Neiman's posse, one at a time, slid back down the mountain and to the camp where Thompson and

Strang were holding the horses, leaving Hoy's body behind. The group of men, with heavy hearts and no choice, left on horseback for the Bassett ranch, leading Hoy's horse.

On their solemn journey, the group headed to pick up Bassett and Vaughn, when they were met by Vaughn riding toward them. He told the sheriff that he and Bassett had observed a lone rider who stopped and fired three shots in the air as he headed out of the mountain range. Waiting a few minutes, he fired again. Believing this was a signal to the outlaws, Vaughn and Bassett rode down to the valley below and in a friendly, leisurely way, approached the man. Bassett recognized the man as John Jack "Judge" Bennett, who was involved in the death of Willie Strang. Vaughn let the sheriff know of the scheme he and Bassett had quickly concocted. In a friendly gesture, Bassett invited the "stranger" to the Bassett ranch for the night. Bennett, accepting the invitation, left with Bassett, as Vaughn explained he would soon follow. Josie later talked about her brother Eb's experience with Bennett:

> Well, my brother Eb was just a big boy then, about seventeen, and he was scared to death of Bennett. Bennett was kind and pleasant to Eb and Eb was to him, and they went home to Bassett's. My father had the post office and he sold tobacco and little things like that. So Bennett said, "We're all out of tobacco," and that made Eb more scared than ever. He thought, "We! Who are 'we?' Wonder who the other people are."

Meanwhile, Neiman and the rest of the posse rode hard to reach the Bassett ranch ahead of Bassett and Bennett. This was accomplished as Bennett's horse was obviously worn out and he and Bassett rode at a slower pace. When Bassett and Bennett finally arrived at the ranch, Eb Bassett corralled the horses while Bennett approached the ranch house.

Inside the Bassett home, Josie Bassett McKnight watched the arrival of her younger brother through the kitchen window. She and her two young sons had been staying at the ranch for safety after McKnight joined the posse. Josie was baking a large batch of cookies when Bennett walked in. He checked his gun at the door which was customary and Josie invited him to have a seat at the table and offered him some of her warm cookies.

As Bennett was enjoying the cookies, deputy sheriff Ethan Farnham walked in. Farnham addressed the man asking if his name was John Bennett. Bennett replied in the affirmative. Farnham then ordered the man on his feet. As Bennett stood, Farnham showed him the arrest warrant for cattle stealing and told him to put his hands up. Over 60 years later, Josie Bassett McKnight recalled the incident:

> I had quit baking cookies to listen to what was going on. I was so scared. I could hardly speak, I was so scared. I thought, "Now if he's got a six-shooter he'll kill Farnham," but he had set his gun down at the back door when he came in. So he held his hands up high and Farnham arrested him, put the handcuffs on him and he didn't make much fuss about it. He swore and made a lot of threats about what he would do when he got loose. He was an impudent looking man.

Farnham took his prisoner to Herb Bassett's post office at Lodore, not far from the Bassett ranch, which also served as a temporary jail when needed. Farnham handcuffed Bennett to a cot and guarded him. Bennett's verbal assaults against Farnham only increased. Josie later said: "He carried on like a gray wolf. You never heard such terrible yells and screams and swearing. We could hear him from the kitchen, hearing him carrying on that way."

The following day, March 2, 1898, near the noon hour, seven masked men entered the temporary jail and leveled a shotgun at Farnham and took his keys, while others moved toward Bennett. They threw a gunny sack over Bennett's head, removed the handcuffs from the cot and placed them on his wrists. While one of the men guarded Farnham, the masked men then took Bennett out of his jail cell and to the adjacent Bassett ranch. At the ranch the men removed Bennett's handcuffs, shackled his legs and arms, and led him to the ten-foot high corral gatepost. Bennett was placed on a buckboard, where a noose was placed around his neck, the knot properly placed behind his right ear. The free end of the rope was then thrown over one of the pine gateposts. The masked men, in a swift motion, then drove the buckboard out from under Bennett. However, the drop was too short to break Bennett's neck and he swung in the air for nearly four minutes before his body finally slumped in the cold mountain air. In his memoirs, J. S. Hoy wrote of the incident:

> Bassitt told me he did not see Bennett hung—that he remained close in his room, not even looking out the window, nor come out until after Bennett was dead and casted away and all was quiet—Bassett did not want his name mixed up in the terrible deed. He could prove by every man there that he took no part in hanging a man, without trial, a man against whom in accusation had been brought. He was safe, the men who asked him to make a hangman's noose, would not dare say anything as they would incriminate themselves. Bassett had been a soldier during the civil war, afterwards and before coming west we [he] had been a clerk in a district cout in Arkansas, two professions that enabled him to know just what to do and what not to in a case of hanging a man—knew all that was done, saw it all but could prove by forty men that he was not even an innocent bystander to say nothing about being an active, one might say one of the leaders in the brutal savage, murdering affair—them and three or four others equally guilty—with Bassett, who could have stifled it by saying a word, not saying anything about the men that did the works, the men led on by Jim unknowingly and as the Judge says, "May God have mercy on your souls."

Josie Bassett McKnight later recalled: "I cooked dinner for the men who lynched Jack Bennett. At the time I didn't know what they'd done. After dinner I went outdoors to hang some dish towels on the clothesline, and there he was, swinging from the corral gate."

The Bassett buggy, with Judge Bennett in the back, was pulled out from Bennett and he was hanged from the Bassett corral post. *Museum of Northwest Colorado*

According to Brown's Park historian, John Rolfe Burroughs, who interviewed Josie about a year before her death, she named three of the masked men as Harry Hindle, Lilton Lyons, and Jim Warren. When asked who the others were, Josie "pled forgetfulness with a twinkle in her eye."

Following dinner the men again donned their masks and returned to where Farnham was being held. They then released him and rode away from the Bassett ranch. Farnham left his temporary prison and found Bennett hanging from the Bassett ranch gatepost. He cut down the body and dragged it up the draw above the ranch house. He then wrapped the body in a blanket, dug a shallow grave, and placed the body of John "Jack" Bennett in the grave.

After he covered the grave, Farnham placed rocks over it in an effort to deter the coyotes. Years later, Crawford McKnight, the older son of Josie and Jim McKnight, was interviewed by John Rolfe Burroughs. He said he and his younger brother didn't believe that there really was a body in that spot above their grandfather's ranch. Crawford said he was about 14 when he and younger brother, Amos "Chick" Herbert filled with curiosity, decided to find out for themselves if the legendary lynching story was true. They took a pick and shovel from their grandfather's ranch and walked up the draw behind the house to the grave site.

> "Chick and I dug down two or three feet. I was swinging the pick and when it hit what seemed to be a hollow place, and when I raised the pick there was a skull on the point. Believe me, we scraped that skull back in the hole and covered it up in a hurry. We must have been a trifle pale around the gills when we went back to the house, because Granddad said, "Well boys, did you find anything?" We allowed as how we had, and were satisfied that the hanging really had taken place.

Following the murder of his brother, Jesse S. Hoy wrote a letter to the *Denver Post*, expressing the seriousness of the outlaw element. Unfortunately, the letter wasn't published until nearly a week later, after the outlaw episode had concluded with a successful arrest. Hoy's letter ran in the March 11, 1898, issue: "One or two men on the trail of a criminal will succeed where 100 men will be sure to fail. They must be hunted down like wild animals, once on their trail stay on it, camp on it until the scoundrels are run down, and there are men who will do it, men just as brave, as cunning and as determined as the outlaws themselves."

A few members of the posse retrieved the body of Valentine S. Hoy. Francis "Frank" Willis, who would later marry Ann Bassett, wrote of the incident in his unpublished memoir, *Confidentially Told:* "Jim McKnight and his assistants delivered Hoy's body at the Bassett ranch and went to help the trailing posse."

The community of Brown's Park came together. With the murder of her husband, Julia Hoy would have to raise her two children, Valentine S. Hoy II and Neva Blair, on her own. Within 18 months Julia Hoy would remarry. As for escaped convicts David Lant and Harry Tracy, Sheriff Neiman and his deputy sheriff, Ethan Farnham continued their search. The *Rock Springs Miner* newspaper reported the story in the March 10, 1898, issue, concluding with the statement: "There is no doubt that the murderers will be shot or lynched as soon as captured."

The murder of Valentine Hoy had brought a new round of willing posse members, including Isom Dart, and again, Joe Davenport and Jim McKnight. The day after the lynching Neiman split his posse in two parties, sending each to watch both exit points of Douglas Mountain. Meanwhile, Neiman, along with Eb Bassett, Tom Davenport, Pete Dillman, Ed "Longhorn" Thompson,

Judge Bennett was buried in a shallow grave on a hill behind the Bassett family ranch.
Museum of Northwest Colorado

and Jerry Murray of the Utah posse, left the Bassett ranch, heading toward the stage road near the Snake River. Neiman left his group sending them to watch for the outlaws in case they crossed the river or waylaid the stage. Neiman and Eb Bassett then backtracked to the Bassett ranch in an effort to hold the stage at the Bassett ranch. Dillman, Murray, and Thompson continued on. It was not long before they found a campsite where the fugitives had stayed. There the posse discovered a gruesome sight. The remains of a horse were found. The outlaws had evidently cut out portions of the horse flesh for consumption. Deputy Sheriff Farnham soon happened upon the party and pressed on after the outlaws.

At a point of five or six miles south of Powder Springs,

and near one of the Davenport sheep ranches, Farnham, using field glasses, spotted the three fugitives sitting on a hill. Farnham and his posse rode toward them. As the men saw the horseman approaching, they rose from their seated position. When the posse were within range, Farnham yelled to the men to halt. The three men ran off in the opposite direction. As the posse quicken their pace after the men, Farnham again ordered the men to stop. Johnson obeyed the order, turning toward the posse with his hands in the air. Lant and Tracy ran toward a hollow where they disappeared from sight. Joe Davenport recalled the capture of the escaped convicts in an interview in the March 1, 1929, issue of the *Rock Springs Rocket*:

> We then incautiously surrounded Tracy and Lant when they might have dropped all five of us. We did not realize what a desperado we had to deal with. They took refuge in a depression in the snow. I alighted from my horse, crawling among the greasewood until I saw Tracy's head sticking up. I didn't shoot. Lant, realizing that he was trapped, started to rise in order to surrender. But the dare-devil Tracy was gamey. He pointed his weapon at Lant and shouted, "Get down there, you blankety-blank blank." Lant then dropped back as Tracy shouted at us, "We'll tell you fellows we're quitting. But we want protection. We don't want to be strung up." After we guaranteed them safety, Lant appeared first with hands aloft. His feet broke through the snow as he approached, and he fell. Pete Swanson, thinking it was a ruse, shot as Lant, but missed him. Tracy then reluctantly appeared, but with his gun in his belt. Knowing the man was desperate, Farnham took a quick shot at him on the spur of the moment, but also missed. It surprised the fearless outlaw, and he could not restrain his anger, but shouted, "You're a fine bunch of cowards, firing at a man with his hands in the air." We still didn't know we had such a noted criminal as Tracy until someone recognized him later. "Gents," he said, "give me a cup of coffee, a fresh horse, and twenty-five yards head start, and I won't bother you no more."

Of course Farnham declined the request, handcuffed the men and the posse set out for the Rock Springs-Brown's Park road. In an ironic twist of fate in this entire outlaw episode, the posse encountered J. S. Hoy and Willis Rouf on horseback. Following the riders was 12-year-old Felix Meyers driving a buckboard containing a wooden coffin with the remains of Valentine Hoy. The group was en route to Rock Springs where they would ship the body by train to the family home in Fremont, Nebraska. However, Deputy Sheriff Farnham, while sympathetic to Hoy's situation, insisted that Hoy, as the police magistrate for Brown's Park, return with the posse to oversee the trial of Johnson, Lant, and Tracy. Understandably, J. S. Hoy was quite upset at the turn of events. Again, Joe Davenport, in the same newspaper interview, related the angry exchange: "Which one of you men killed my brother? "Well one of us here did it,' Tracy replied defiantly. We continued on down Irish and Bull Canyons to Bassett's ranch. As we approached the house, Farnham sent me ahead to tell the remainder of the posse waiting there that we had our men, and to keep cool and not get excited."

J. S. Hoy later wrote:

> After their capture, Lant and Tracy related their experiences. They were hidden under the rimrock as the officers had thought, and had their guns ready to kill when their pursuers should approach. They were going to allow the officers to approach close enough to make sure of their aim, and planned to get the entire posse, which would easily have been possible. Then with the horses of the officers, they planned to escape out of the country.
>
> The mountain sets in the angle formed by Bear and Green rivers, and there was no escape ahead; that they would circle and go back seemed probable. Neiman, Farnham, Hoy, McKnight and Pidgeon followed the fresh trail up the mountain side, in places so steep that it was necessary for the officers to [take] hold of trees and projections to pull themselves up. The officers talked only in whispers and had their guns ready for instant use. They were following up a narrow gulch, and presently came to a

great rock which would have barred further progress along the path they were traveling, except that the rock had split apart, leaving a crevice just wide enough for a man to crawl through.

Valentin S. Hoy walked ahead to the crevice of the rock, twenty feet distant. Instantly there were two rifle reports in quick succession and the curling smoke from behind the rock showed that the hunted men were driven to bay there, and with every advantage were intent on murdering all that advanced. Valentine Hoy crumpled up on the snow, which rapidly turned crimson with his lifes blood. He was shot through the heart, and his death was instantanious. He was a pioneer of the park, owner of much land and many cattle, and was a brave and upright man. Exposed to the fire of an entrenched enemy having every advantage and only a few feet distant, the four officers threw themselves behind rocks and trees and for more than an hour, the two parties faced each other with every nerve tense. Once Tracy, peering around the rock, his dark, crafty face malignant and cruel, and Neiman swung his gun into position, but the outlaw dodged back. It was an instant that the outlaw and the sheriff gazed into each others faces, but they were so close to each other that when they again met, at the time of the capture, each recognized the other and Tracy remarked, with that cruel grin that was characteristic of him, "I've seen you before, sheriff." McKnight saw, or thought he saw, a glimpse of one of the outlaws, and fired a shot at him."

The *Craig Courier* covered the story in the March 12, 1898, issue with the largest typeset headline ever used by the editor:

OUTLAWRY ENDED IN BROWN'S PARK

Bennett, One Of The Powder Springs Gang, Lynched And Johnson The Murderer Of Strang, In Jail! V.S. Hoy Murdered. Only Six Feet Away From The Man Who Fired the Fatal Shot All The Bandits Caught Tracy And Lant, Now Prisoners Of This County, Are Escaped Convicts Credit Due Routt's Officers

J. S. Hoy later added details to the apprehension of the outlaws and murderers of his brother:

> The officers opened fire and shouted a demand for surrender. Johnstone threw up his hands and walked toward the officers and surrendered. Lant and Tracy reached the gulch, while the officers circled and continued to fire. Presently Lant and Tracy came out of hiding with hands up in token of surrender. This was six or seven miles south of Powder springs. Tracy and Johnstone had Winchesters and all three men had revolvers. They were taken before Justice of the Peace J.S. Hoy, a brother of the murdered man, for preliminary examinations.

The hearing was held in the large living room of the Bassett home, with Justice of the Peace for the Precinct of Lodore, Routt County, J. S. Hoy presiding. The room was filled with witnesses and bystanders, including Herb and Eb Bassett, and Jim and Josie McKnight. Hoy, in remarkable composure given he was presiding over a legal matter which resulted in the death of his brother, held the hearing from the head of the Bassett family dining table. The accused, Lant and Tracy, were stoic during the proceedings, although Tracy displayed an air of contempt from time to time. J. S. Hoy wrote: "The testimony of Neiman and Johnstone was taken in writing and is now in the file of the District court, bearing out the main parts of the above narrative."

Following the hearing, Justice of the Peace J. S. Hoy issued the following ruling, dated March 5, 1898:

> Office of the Justice of the Peace.
> Ladore, Colo., March 5, 1898.
>
> On the above date, P. L. Johnstone David Lant and Harry Tracy were brought before me by the Sheriff of Routt

County charged with the killing of Valentine S. Hoy on the afternoon of March 1, 1898. I examined the three prisoners, the testimony of P. L Johnson being in writing. The other two testified, but their testimony was not reduced to writing. I also examined Sheriff Charles Neiman, E. A. Farnham, and James McKnight. To me, the evidence taken and the circumstances surrounding the killing of Valentine S. Hoy was sufficient to bind the prisoners over to the district court without bail, and they were accordingly remanded to the custody of the Sheriff to be confined in the county jail until the decision so rendered by due course of law, except in the case of P. L. Johnstone, who was turned over to the custody of Deputy United States Marshal Charles Laney, who claimed Johnstone on a writ of requisition from the Governor of Wyoming. Mittimus remanding Lant and Tracy to the county jail contains the names of the four principal witnesses in the prosecution, to wit: Charles Neiman, E. A. Farnham, James McKnight, and J. S. Hoy.

J. S. Hoy
J.P. Ladore Precinct.

Later that night, when Justice of the Peace Jesse S. Hoy's ruling reached the citizens of Brown's Park, a large group of men arrived at the Bassett ranch. According to Brown's Park historian, John Rolfe Burroughs, "It was the largest congregation of law officers and law-abiding citizens ever seen in those parts." J. S. Hoy wrote:

A large posse arrived from Uintah county, Utah, and that night at the Bassett ranch, there were sixty men to be fed. Of course there were no sleeping accommodations for that many, so they built a big bon fire in the yard, and most of them dozed about the fire. The prisoners were kept in the bunk house, shackled, and with two men constantly on guard. Several times during the night a movement was started to lynch the prisoners and a leader was all that remained up all night mingling with the men and urging them to allow the law to take its course. If he had been less vigilant it might have turned out better in the end.

    With lynching on the minds of many of the men, Sheriff Neiman spent a long night discouraging the men from such an action. At sunrise the following morning, the Wyoming posse left the Bassett ranch with their prisoner, a shackled P. L. Johnson. Sheriff Charles Neiman, cognizant of the lynch mob fever, left the ranch with Lant and Tracy under heavy guard to Hahns Peak and the Routt County jail, traveling along back-country cattle trails. Shortly after arriving at the jail, Lant and Tracy managed to escape, giving Neiman quite a beating in the process. The two were apprehended 24 hours later by Sheriff Neiman at a stage stop near Steamboat Springs. Neiman then requested that the Ninth District Court, under Thomas A. Rucker, transfer the prisoners to the more secure jail at Aspen, the county seat of Pitkin County and the Ninth District Court of the state of Colorado. The transfer of the prisoners was granted and the prisoners were escorted to the Pitkin County jail, where they again managed to escape after beating the jailer nearly to death. Following their escape, the two split up, with Lant disappearing. Tracy made his way to Oregon, continuing in his criminal activities until he was eventually apprehended and sent back to prison, where he killed three guards and escaped again. With the posse closing in, Tracy committed suicide in a rural cornfield in Washington. As for P. L. Johnson, he was tried for the murder of young Willie Strang in a Wyoming court and acquitted of the charge.

    The citizens of Brown Park, believing the outlaw element had been run out of the area, eventually returned to their normal daily ranch life. For Ann Bassett, her life would never be normal again.

CHAPTER NOTES AND SOURCE INFORMATION

Hiram "Hi" Bernard's quotes are from *Confidentially Told*, the unpublished manuscript by Frank Willis. Willis spent the summer of 1917 with Bernard ranging cattle near Green River west of the Bassett ranch.

Warner's description of Charlie Crouse can be found on page 113 of *Last of the Bandit Riders...Revisited.*

Ann's remarks regarding the horse race and Butch Cassidy are found in her then working memoir, *Scars and Two Bars*, published in the *Moffat County Mirror*, April 1, 1943.

Ann's quotes regarding Cassidy and his fellow outlaws are from "Queen Ann of Brown's Park," the *Colorado Magazine*, Volume XXIX October 1952.

Josie's quotes regarding both Butch Cassidy and Matt Warner can be found in her taped interviews, held at the Dinosaur National Monument, Jensen, Utah. Typewritten account is available at the Museum of Northwest Colorado, Craig, Colorado.

Josie's quote regarding Ann's schooling is from her taped interviews held at the Dinosaur National Monument, Jensen, Utah. Typewritten account is available at the Museum of Northwest Colorado, Craig, Colorado.

In Grace McClure's *The Bassett Women*, she refers to the school in Boston as Miss Porter's. It was actually Mrs. Potter's School for Girls, correctly stated in both Burroughs's account and Ann's own memoirs. It is interesting to note that during further research, it was learned that the Porter School for Girls, located in Connecticut, has received numerous calls from researchers. Ann Bassett never attended this institution. Further research revealed that several records of Mrs. Potter's School for Girls were burned in a fire.

Ann's remembrances of her time away at school can be found in "Queen Ann of Brown's Park," the *Colorado Magazine*, in Volume XXIX April 1952.

Burroughs description of Ann Bassett is found on page 221 of *Where the Old West Stayed Young.*

Several writers have speculated on a romantic relationship

between Ann Bassett and Elza Lay. While Ann herself was prone to much exaggeration, reading Ann's own accounts of her relationship with Elza Lay draws no such conclusion.

Ann's description of the Thanksgiving party is from her account published in the *Colorado Magazine*, Volume XXIX.

Many writers have disputed Ann's account of those present at the Thanksgiving party. The year of the event is the primary source of contention. Writers such as William Tennent and Grace McClure (probably from Tennent) have stated, incorrectly, that the event occurred "around" 1895. However, Cassidy was still incarcerated at the Wyoming State Penitentiary. Robert Leroy Parker, alias Butch Cassidy, was released from prison on January 19, 1896. In her accounts of the event, Ann never mentioned a date. The 1895 date used stems from Esther Campbell and carried forward by William Tennent.

In both her published and unpublished memoirs, Ann continuously misspelled the Sundance Kid's given surname, Longabough, as Henry Rhudenbaugh or Harry Roudenbaugh.

Warner's account of how George Leroy Parker, alias "Butch Cassidy," gained his moniker is found in *Last of the Bandit Riders...Revisited*, page 42.

Many historians maintain the nickname came from his one-time employment in a Wyoming butcher shop. This has never been definitively substantiated.

Quotes attributed to Jesse S. Hoy are from his unpublished manuscript and information shared with the author through his great-grandnephew, Valentine Hoy IV.

The James Carl Sizer quote is found in the Routt County National Forest archives.

Josie's quotes are from her taped interviews, located in the Dinosaur National Monument archives. Typewritten account is available at the Museum of Northwest Colorado, Craig, Colorado.

Josie incorrectly identified the ranch as Valentine Hoy's; it was Jesse S. Hoy's ranch.

For Josie's revelation of the masked outlaws, see Burroughs, *Where the Old West Stayed Young*, pg. 165.

In July 1895, new owners of Craig's first newspaper, the

Pantograph, changed the name to the *Craig Courier*. Years later, the paper would merge, becoming the *Empire Courier.*

In the summer of 1917, Frank Willis and Hi Bernard were caring for cattle near the Green River, west of the Bassett ranch. During many conversations with Bernard, Willis began forming a memoir,*Confidentially Told*.

MURDER IN THE PARK

At the age of 19, Ann began a romantic relationship with 32 year-old Madison Matthew Rash, a handsome sandy-haired cowboy and one of her mother's most loyal ranch hands, as well as the former trail boss for the Middlesex outfit, Elizabeth's nemesis. Soon, the two were engaged to be married. Noted Brown's Park historian, John Rolfe Burroughs wrote: "Accentuated by the fact that they were engaged to be married... theirs was the romance of the Northwestern Colorado cattle country."

The *Craig Courier*, dated January 9, 1897, reported a Christmas dinner event, hosted by the J. W. Lowell, Jr. family of Lily Park: "In attendance were the James McKnight family, [Ann's sister, Josie,] Misses Ann Bassett and Blanche Tilton, Messers Sam and Elbert Bassett, and M. M. Rash. They reported a most enjoyable affair, having been entertained with a sumptuous dinner, a Christmas tree, and a very pleasant dance."

In Ann's memoirs, she recounts Rashes history:

He [Rash] was an ex-Texas Ranger and a nephew of Davy Crockett. He had come to Wyoming from Acton, Hood County, Texas, as 'trail boss' of a herd of cattle delivered to the Middlesex Company in 1882. He became range manager for the "G" outfit, which belonged to the Middlesex, and later went to the Circle K, in the same capacity. Rash continued there, employed by Tim Kinney, until his cattle business was changed to sheep. Matt was a number one cow man and was given financial backing by Kinney, to branch out into the cattle business for himself.

He soon established a solid bank credit and frequently negotiated loans of large sums of money through the Rock Springs banks. He bought and sold cattle in three states, Wyoming, Colorado, and Utah. Rash had a wide circle of friends, who held great respect for his word, regarding his character above reproach.

Rash was well respected among the local ranchers. Carl Davidson, in the summers of his teen years, rode many roundups in Brown's Park, from the Cold Spring Mountain range, where Rash lived. Following one particular roundup, in the spring of 1899, John Boyce, of Baggs, Wyoming, and a friend of the Davidson family, paid a visit to his friend, Matt Rash. In the course of conversation, Rash asked Boyce if he happened to know who owned the reversed JJ cattle brand, as he had a steer with that brand in his corral. Boyce informed Rash the brand belonged to the Davidson Ranch on Four Mile Creek. As this was quite some distance from Rash's ranch, Rash soon shipped the steer, by rail, to the Davidson family.

Rash became the first president of the newly formed Brown's Park Cattle Association and helped to establish a dividing line separating the Brown's Park cattle from those of Ora Haley and his Two Bar Ranch and Cattle Company. Haley, a wealthy Wyoming cattle rancher, with ranches in Colorado, including the Yampa River Valley area, had intentions of moving his large herd onto the fertile grazing land of Brown's Park. Haley had recently expanded his ranch at Lay, and moved his headquarters to his new ranch on the eastern edge of Brown's Park, near the Snake River. The registered brand Haley used was two slanted bars **/ /** located on the animal's left hip.

The line Rash and the Brown's Park Cattle Association drew was halfway between the Snake River and Vermilion Creek, a north-south demarcation that managers of the Two Bar Ranch agreed to, for a while. Ann wrote of the new cattle association and Rash's leadership:

This photograph of Tom Horn was taken on a hill in Brown's Park in 1900 - the year Matt Rash and Isom Dart were murdered. *Museum of Northwest Colorado*

Representing our cattle association, he [Rash] interviewed Hi Bernard in the matter of establishing a boundary line between Snake River and Brown's Park. This resulted in an agreement between Bernard and Rash that the hills known as the "Divide," a range of limestone about halfway between Snake River and Vermilion Creek, extending north and south from the Escalante Hills to Douglas Mountain, was to be the western boundary for the Two Bar, and the eastern boundary for the Brown's Park cattle. The arrangement was acceptable to all concerned. There were no fences, so it was necessary to ride Boone Trail and Douglas Mesa to check the drift of the cattle...the Brown's Park cattlemen "pitched" a temporary camp on the Divide, and carried on this line riding during the winter of 1898-1899.

The situation seemed to be satisfactory for both sides when the spring roundup of 1899 occurred, according to Ann, who later recalled:

When the spring round-up was conducted, few strays were found on either side of the divide. Such a logical solution to the problem appeared highly satisfactory—on the surface. The drift control had proved far too efficient to please the Two Bar, or to serve their purpose. But the agreement had been made and Bernard could not back out creditably. Yet the plan was completely cutting off any advance towards the range to the west, coveted by the Two Bar.

Haley hired perhaps the best known cattleman in the southern Wyoming basin, 39 year-old Hiram "Hi" Bernard, to run his newest cattle operation. Bernard began working with cattle in his home state of Texas at the age 12, in an effort to help his family. He herded cattle along the Chisholm Trail on a few cattle drives and then settled in Wyoming, managing various cattle operations prior to being hired by Haley. Bernard enjoyed the freedom that came with working cattle. He later said:

> I was independent, my work suited me. I understood cattle and liked to work with them and wanted to remain free from financial worries. I lived well, kept good and comfortable quarters at the ranches, and put up at the best hotels when I went to the cities. I spent my money as I saw fit among all classes, some of the best, and some of the worst, all of which I found were more or less alike in many respects, just human, with the same human instincts expressed in different ways.

Bernard was proud of the fact that none of the ranches he managed ever went out of business under his control. Bernard once said: "My job was to handle an investment that happened to be cattle. The investment paid a big dividend to the investors. They were satisfied."

Ora Haley, who made just as much money in short-term speculations in the cattle market as he did by owning large cattle companies, trusted Bernard's judgment in both men and cattle. So much so that he gave him a company checkbook to buy cattle, an expense account, and more importantly, land. According to Brown's Park historian, John Rolfe Burroughs: "Hi Bernard made Ora Haley a million dollars in northwestern Colorado that he might just as well have made for himself."

Frank Willis, in his unpublished memoir, *Confidentially Told,* quoted Bernard:

> When small ranch seekers came to squat on our ranges,
> I was not in sympathy with them and used every means
> in my power to move them on, using force if need be.
> Every poor family moving in a covered wagon to settle on
> a lonesome claim, to chuck into a little rough dugout or
> a dirt-covered log shack brought back memories of bed
> bugs, my childhood, and my little sad mother in poverty,
> drudging wearily along and bravely enduring such an
> existence. The thought of struggling individuals going the
> hard way and bucking against odds they could not conquer
> was hateful, and turned me sour.

Bernard, acting on Haley's behalf, purchased the B. F. Majors-Sainsbury ranch on the lower Snake River, just east of the Park. Ann recounted the incident that would heavily impact the ranchers of Brown's Park:

> Hi Bernard, manager for the Haley Two Bar cattle outfit,
> with ranches near Craig, Colorado, bought the Ben Majors
> and Sainsbury Ranches on the lower Snake River, thirty
> miles from Brown's Park. Soon after the transfers of the
> ranches, several thousand head of Two Bar cattle were
> driven into Routt County and turned on summer range.
> The intent of Haley to occupy all of the summer and
> winter range of the county was clearly demonstrated.
> There were hundreds of miles of range outside of the Park,
> yet we with our small herds, isolated in the west end of the

natural drift, and with less snow and plenty of feed were again in danger of becoming overrun by the big herds of cattle owned by non-residents.

Hi Bernard had a different perspective:

Our company ran a roundup and a mess wagon, and provided a simple, economical way for small cattle owners to handle their stock. We furnished everything, and did most of the work. All they had to do was get their stock after it was gathered, at no expense to them. I went into Brown's Park to make similar arrangements, and got cold-shouldered. My offer was rejected with ceremonial courtesy. On that mission I did not meet Ann Bassett, but I received a letter from her soon afterwards, advising that neither I nor the Haley outfit were desirable; and when if necessary for me to visit Brown's Park, would I please confine myself to road travel, for the tracks of Two Bar horses and cattle were obnoxious. That impertinent demand was not in the form of a joke. Not by any means, it was an open defiance straight from the shoulder. That demand still rings in my ears, very pleasantly at times.

Ann recalled that era a bit differently:

Up to the time of Bernard's buying the Snake River ranches for the Two Bar, no cattle belonging to that outfit had crossed the ridge into Brown's Park. They had not fully stocked the range, nor found winter feed near the ranches at Lay Creek. Hi Bernard, whose ability to judge cattle and ranges was perhaps unsurpassed, saw the benefit to be derived by complete control of the entire open range between the Utah line on the west, Wyoming on the north; and east to Hahn's Peak; comprising an area of hundreds of square miles of cow range. Brown's Park cattle owners had only a few thousand head of cattle but held by right of range custom of that period, one of the finest winter ranges in the West. These cow men and women could contribute nothing to the large herds, and they would not yield and become absorbed, because they were prosperous and deeply rooted in a business they understood.

And then Haley set in motion a series of events aimed to take over the small ranches and gain control of the rich grazing land in the Park. Bernard assigned a few of his hired hands to ride the line, keeping an eye on any rustlers.

Haley had also joined with four other large cattle companies in Routt County to form the Snake River Stock Growers Association. The objective was to gain control of Brown's Park grazing land and drive out the few sheep ranchers in the area. The group included Haley's Two Bar operation, the Pierce-Reef Sevens ranch, the Yampa Valley Livestock's Two Circle Bar, and Charlie Ayers' Bar Ell Seven ranch. Also included in this group was John Coble of Wyoming's Swan Cattle operations. These men established their own "cattleman's committee," similar to the Wyoming Stock Growers Association based in Cheyenne. The large cattle barons considered anyone who contested their control of the open range a menace, or worse, a rustler. The committee was soon enlarged to include five more Routt County ranchers.

During a secret meeting the cattle ranchers each agreed to pay one hundred dollars a month to Charlie Ayer, who would then pay a private stock inspector, ostensibly to procure evidence of rustling in the Brown's Park area. Hiram "Hi' Bernard, ranch foreman for Ora Haley, who attended the secret meeting, later recounted: "John Cobel

Matt Rash was found dead in his cabin on Cold Spring Mountain on July 10, 1900.
Museum of Northwest Colorado

offered a solution to the problem that would wipe out range menace permanently . He would contact a man from the Pinkerton Detective Agency. A man who could be relied on to do the job no questions asked."

In fact, the man hired was none other than Tom Horn, a known killer for hire in Wyoming. Among the men who agreed to hiring Horn were John Coble, Tim Kinney, the former owner of the Circle K Ranch, where Matt Rash once worked, and Ora Haley of the Two Bar ranches. A hired killer was an abhorrent thought to most folks, but apparently not to the large cattle ranch owners in the tri-state area.

Nor did it seem to be a problem for Hi Bernard. Bernard was in Craig on May 6, 1900, for what he thought was a secret meeting with Tom Horn and another man known as Mexican Pete. The men, meeting in the local livery stable, were unaware of the presence of a man by the name of George Banks. As Banks innocently overheard the conversation between the men, he kept his presence concealed. Years later Banks wrote of the conversation he overheard:

> I heard Mr. Bernard say, "Now we have got to get rid of those thieves," and he says to Mr. Hicks [Horn], "You kill Rash and that negro and Thompson and notify Ann and Elbert Bassett and Joe Davenport to leave the country and you can get your pay." Mr. Bernard pulled some paper out of his pocket and [said], "Here is some men we want watched." He handed one small sheet of paper to Hicks and one to [Mexican] Pete.

If Banks's account is accurate, it proves Bernard not only knew of the hiring of Tom Horn, which he later would admit, although privately, but more damning to his otherwise stellar reputation that he had a hand in the intimidation acts of Horn, but not necessarily in the murders that were about to occur. A few days after this incident, someone fired a bullet at Banks. The shooter missed his mark and Banks ran for cover. Banks reported the attempted assassination to Routt County Sheriff, Ethan Allen

Farnham. In an interview with the *Steamboat Pilot* on December 5, 1900, Farnham had this to say regarding the shooting incident, "It was probably a stray bullet from a chicken hunter."

This ludicrous statement would cause many in Brown's Park to wonder if the sheriff was in the pocket of the cattle barons, who were trying to drive them out. In the meantime, Hi Bernard did his job well for Haley and the Two Bar. He swore out several complaints against ranchers in the Park, accusing them of rustling Two Bar cattle. The *Craig Courier* of June 18, 1898, reported:

> Mr. Bernard has had certain people under surveillance for some months and the loss of about thirty head of cattle was traced to four of the suspected parties. Two of the men arrested are Bob Lockhard and Bill Laney. The names of the other two rustlers could not be learned. The arrest was made by the sheriff of Sweetwater County, Wyoming, at the headquarters of the gang, a ranch on Salt Wells Creek, about 25 miles north of the Wyoming line from Brown's Park. These four men are supposed to have been doing a thriving business by killing beef and marketing it in Rock Springs.

In August, Bernard had also sworn out a complaint against N. N. Ferris, who was arrested on suspicion of cattle rustling. The August 20, 1898 issue of the *Craig Courier* reported the case against Ferris had been dismissed for lack of evidence. As was the case against Bill Laney. Again, the *Craig Courier* would report in the October 7, 1899 issue that in the case of the "People versus Laney," the jury voted not guilty.

The smaller ranch owners of Brown's Park were not intimidated by such actions. To the contrary, anger brewed, especially within Ann Bassett.

As the large cattle barons, with their new self-imposed power, attempted to force a takeover in Brown's Park, many ranchers struggled to survive amidst the intimidation. Ann Bassett was not one to be bullied and soon found herself in the middle of Colorado's largest range war. While she struggled to hold onto her family's ranch, several of the larger cattle companies tried to drive her out. Ann refused to sell and dug in for a fight. She was described as "a bold young woman that all the cowboys liked and respected."

In the summer of 1899, Ann learned of some 20 head of cattle that had strayed beyond the boundary lines agreed to by Rash and the Brown's Park Cattle Association, and the large cattle companies. Joe Davenport, a local rancher and friend of the Bassetts, had discovered the cattle, with the brand VD connected. Ann later described the situation:

> In June, 1899, twenty-one head of young cattle branded VD connected strayed from the north and lodged among a band of Tom Davenport's sheep in Willow Creek Canyon. Joe Davenport looked the cattle over and saw from the brand that they did not belong locally, the VD was new to this particular range. He let the cattle pass through the sheep herd and they drifted down the canyon. Before leaving camp for the Davenport ranch, Joe instructed the Mexican herder to get the names of any one inquiring about the cattle, and to tell them to see Joe Davenport about such stock. When he returned to the sheep camp he was told by the herder that Charley Ward had been there to ask about cattle, and said that a bunch of his had strayed from Clay Basin. Ward was a person of doubtful reputation who had owned nothing but a saddle and pack horse during the few years he had been in or around Brown's Park. He was not a cow puncher and his interest in cattle, or his suddenly becoming a cow man was a decidedly unusual condition.

Ann is mistaken as to the date of this incident. While the cattle had been in the area nearly all summer, for whatever reason, most likely in preparation for the upcoming roundup in October, the Davenports did not inspect the cattle until September. Joe Davenport traveled to Brown's Park in search of Matt Rash, president of the Brown's Park Cattle Association, in an effort to alert him of strange cattle. Expecting to find him at the Bassett ranch, he stopped there. Rash was not present, but Ann was. Ann continued her account:

> Joe told me of Ward's visit and statement that he owned cattle which had strayed, the "lost" cattle struck a bright spark of interest. "Those strays did not get into this country by themselves," I declared positively. "Ward stole them, and probably from some place in Utah, since they are headed that way, probably trying to get back to their home range. Yip-pee! I've got a wonderful idea," I exclaimed. "The poor cattle are homesick, let's give 'em a leg over the river. We will demonstrate on those VD cattle."

Ann Bassett was about to commit her first act of retaliation against what she supposed was the subtle encroachment by the large cattle owners. It was an impulsive stunt, conducted without knowing the facts, and when the facts were later known, it became something she had to conceal, at all costs, from her fiancé Matt Rash. But in the moment, Ann was determined to carry out her scheme. Ann wrote:

> Joe Davenport wasn't enthusiastic about my impulsive plan. Nor did he view the situation from my angle. But my determination over-ruled his reluctance to take such action. "Don't stand there looking at me," I told him, "drag it to the pasture and run in a fresh string, so Aunty Thompson and father won't get their heads together and decide 'Ann's up to something again.'"
>
> And away we galloped, to stretch our hard-twist ropes in what I believed to be a worthy cause. We found the cattle about four miles west of the Davenport Ranch, near Green River. The river was bank full and over-flowing. There [we] tried skills at roping big game in the open.
>
> We spent the night at the Davenport ranch, and hurried back to the cattle for more entertainment. It was great sport to watch them swim the Green River at the old

113

Parsons ford, and see them land in good shape on the west bank near the deserted Parsons ranch, and over the Utah line.

After that swimming stunt, the cattle disappeared from Brown's Park, not one of them ever straying back. Nor was Ward seen afterward. He departed, where and how was never made known.

Meanwhile, the mysterious disappearance of the VD cattle raised concern among several local ranchers, including Matt Rash. Rash and a few men from the Brown's Park Cattle Association had begun a search for the cattle in late September. As the news spread, Charlie Ayers traveled from Baggs, Wyoming, to help with the search. Arriving at Craig, Ayers acquired a fresh horse at the livery stables, but was immediately thrown from the horse. Suffering a broken hip and several broken bones, Ayers was no longer able to help with the search. The *Craig Courier* carried the story of Ayers' injuries and his forced withdrawal from the VD cattle search. This raised another mystery: Why did C. E. Ayers feel the need to travel from Baggs, Wyoming, to search for 20 head of cattle he had no affiliation with? Or did he? Another mystery surrounding the VD cattle lingered, at least in the mind of Carl Davidson, as he later wrote:

Now I will have to tell you what I know about the VD cows. There were two brothers, John and Dow Doty. They had ranches between Baggs and Rawlins. One was at the Willows which was halfway between Baggs and Rawlins and was the halfway stage station. The other ranch was east of there on Cow Creek.

They ran a good sized bunch of horses for some time. Their brand was VD connected. The spring of 1899 they went to Vernal, Utah, bought a bunch of cows and calves and trailed them back. They crossed the Green River on the bridge at Bridgeport which was the Charley Crouse ranch. They stopped there for noon, then drove off and left 23 head of cows and calves. The cows were branded but the calves were not. Crouse told me the cows were there all summer. He saw them every day. Then sometime in September Isom Dart and Queen Ann drove them down... That was the last Crouse ever saw of them.

Why did Doty go and leave them there? And why didn't they go back and get them?

After the October roundup, the mystery of the missing VD cattle seemed to die down. Then, in "mid-winter," as Ann writes, she learned she had been wrong in her original assessment regarding the VD cattle. Ann wrote:

As cow technicians we had blundered, for the cattle had not come from Utah. In mid-winter Joe Davenport wrote me and said:

"The VD cattle are in the picture again. Mat Rash has been notified that the cattle of such description and brand were stolen on upper Snake River near Baggs, Wyoming, and they were traced to Vermillion Canyon."

In the letter Joe asked me if he should tell Mat Rash what we knew about the VD cattle? My answer was, "NO, and do not so much as imply to Sam Bassett or Mat Rash, that we ever heard of that stuff. If you do it will be 'chaps' for us."

Ann now had to figure her way out of the first crime she had committed, and more importantly, in her mind, keep it secret so that her fiancé would never learn the truth. Ann continued her tale of deceit:

It was evident we were in bad for failing to give the information when Joe discovered the cattle. I had intervened and now months had passed since the VD cattle were crossed over the river and gone in the opposite direction from where they belonged. My "wonderful idea" was giving off echoes! The situation was grave indeed. Our next move was to confide in Buffalo Jack—we could trust him to keep a secret—we made a clean confession of our guilt, and asked his advice (it was our fixed habit not to seek his council until mired to the neck by some of our many imbecilities.) Buffalo Jack admonished us for such petty mischief, but saw no foundation for great anxiety. He reasoned that it would not help matters to say anything at that time, for the cattle were branded, they could not be lost. They would show up sometime, and would then be reported.

Ann, believing this episode was behind her, and her secret was safe from Matt Rash, focused her attention on what she considered to be obvious intrusion by the cattle barons, and particularly the Two Bar outfit into Brown's Park. She began riding along the eastern edge of the Divide, always carrying a rifle. She would shoot any Two Bar animal wandering over the Divide.

The fight over land became personal when Ann's fiancé, Matt Rash, was shot dead at his cabin. The former employee of the large Middlesex Cattle Company was obstinately believed by the "cattleman's committee" to be a cattle rustler. The reality is most likely that as the president of the Brown's Park Cattle Association, Rash was instrumental in forming a sizable opposition to the cattle barons and needed to be eliminated.

In April 1900, a stranger had arrived in Brown's Park giving his name as James Hicks and his occupation as ranch hand. He made his rounds in an unassuming manner, calling on various ranch owners including the Bassett ranch. Josie Bassett McKnight later recalled the incident:

> I knew Tom Horn [alias Hicks] when he first came to the country. He came to the Bassett's place. I lived at Willow Creek then. I was home when he came. He was a suspicious looking man. He pretended to be a horse buyer and wanted to stay there at the Bassetts. And my brother [Sam] said, "Why yes, you can stay here, we have horses to sell." He [Horn] wasn't a horse buyer atal. After supper, I said to Sam, "I don't believe he's a horse buyer, I think he's a horse

thief, something wrong about him." Well, he stayed there and we all went up to look at the Bassett horses, eighteen miles up there. He was riding my brother's horse. He couldn't handle a rope better than I could. He was there for another purpose.

Horn, alias James Hicks, must have realized his ruse was not working with the Bassett family. It is questionable whether he knew of Ann Bassett's relation and engagement to Matt Rash. Nevertheless, Horn moved on to Rash's cabin, ostensibly looking for work. Rash hired Hicks as a ranch hand. The two were nearly inseparable as they rode together working on the ranch. On a typical day herding cattle near Cold Spring Mountain, the two happened upon Isom Dart who was butchering a young bull. Both men saw the brand on the animal which belonged to Sam Spicer. Rash was shocked. He and Dart exchanged heated words as Hicks watched. Hicks had gained, or fabricated, according to Hi Bernard, the needed information he was after regarding rustlers in the area.

Allen G. Wallihan, owner of the stage station at Lay, Colorado, southeast of Brown's Park, met the man called Hicks. Wallihan said: "I didn't like him. He came here several times looking for some boots on the mail and when they did not arrive he got mad. My wife had lived all her life on the frontier, and she was not afraid of God, man, or devil, but she said: 'That man Hicks is a bad man.'"

Ann Bassett, with her female intuition, along with her sister, Josie, mistrusted Hicks from the start, and soon came to the conclusion that he was not who he said he was. Ann continued:

Representing himself [Hicks] as a ranchman from New Mexico in search of a location for a small cattle set-up, he put up as a guest at the home ranch of Matt Rash, where every courtesy was extended. When the spring roundup started, it soon became evident that he was not a cowpuncher, and he was given a job as roundup cook. The roundup was in full swing when I came home from

117

school and joined the work as usual. His bragging of having been a great Indian fighter, and his descriptive account of slaughters he had accomplished single-handed, [was] extremely obnoxious to me. "Hicks" seemed to recognize the "Indian sign" as unfavorable to his best interests, and he immediately removed his carcass from the roundup. That was the one and only time I ever saw Tom Horn, alias James Hicks.

Ann was prone to exaggeration in her many writings and this is a prime example. Tom Horn, alias James Hicks, arrived in Brown's Park in 1900. Ann says she attended the roundup when she returned from school. In fact, Ann returned to the Park after her schooling in 1895, five years before Horn arrived in Brown's Park. Nevertheless, Ann later wrote: "I did not take kindly to the [man.] His bragging that he had been a great Indian fighter, his boastful, descriptive accounts of the human slaughter he had accomplished single-handed, were exceedingly obnoxious to me. I emphasized this point with vehemence in several heated arguments."

Years later when Ann wrote her memoirs, she included additional information regarding James Hicks, alias Tom Horn. The missing VD cattle and subsequent search by Matt Rash and others was still on-going. Ann wrote:

> The owner of the VD cattle was not a member of the "inner circle" and was not told of the circumstances surrounding the disappearance of his cattle, therefore, he was chiefly concerned about their whereabouts. He had written to well-known cattle men in various parts of the country, explaining his loss, asking them to be on the lookout for his stock. Mat Rash received one of such letter, and he was making every effort to get some trace of the cattle. He did not think of his guest, Mr. Hicks, as a suspect, nor of his being involved in the missing cattle. Mat Rash had no suspicion I had fallen into a trap by crossing the VD cattle over the river.

The trap Ann mentions was of her own making. It should be remembered that pushing the VD cattle into the Green River was her idea, despite the objections of Joe Davenport. Was Ann trying to justify the action in her later years? Or was she speaking of "the trap" she found herself in by concealing the act from Matt Rash, her fiancé who also happened to be the president of the Brown's Park Cattle Association? Ann continues with the following account:

> To promote his criminal purpose Tom Horn, assisted by his spawn [Charley] Ward, had stolen the VD cattle at Baggs, Wyoming, and smuggled them over the winter range to Clay Basin. He [Horn] reported to the Snake River association that he had detected the theft, and incriminated several Brown's Park cattlemen, among them Jim Mac Knight and Mat Rash. It had been Horn's intention to sell the stolen cattle to a butcher in Rock Springs.
>
> While Horn was in Rock Springs to negotiate the sale, Ward had carelessly permitted the cattle to get away. When Horn returned from his trip, he assumed a manner of indifference and made no close inquiry. On learning that Mat Rash was investigating the whereabouts of the VD cattle, he was undisturbed. No suspicion had been cast at Horn.

How Ann learned this information, if true, is unclear. It could not have been from Matt Rash, as he was still conducting the search at the time of his murder and had no idea of her involvement. It is doubtful she learned it from Hi Bernard, as Bernard not only knew of Horn's hiring by Ora Haley, through the Snake River Association, but even secretly assisted Horn on occasion. It is also quite possible, given Ann Bassett's propensity for exaggeration, that she saw an opportunity to fabricate a tale around her unlawful deed regarding the VD cattle and the murderous acts of Tom Horn. Nevertheless, Ann continued with her account:

Rash failed in his efforts to locate the cattle. and there the matter rested. To add up later. The fact was revealed several years afterward, that Horn suspected Ward of having outwitted him in the disposal of the cattle. This partly upset his double-barreled scheme, which was to sell the cattle at a profit to himself, and fasten the crime upon the Brown's Parkers. He would then murder for an additional sum of money, the men he had accused of the theft. The scheme worked out, in part. Within a short time Mat Rash was found dead in his summer cabin, from gun shots fired at close range.

Hi Bernard had an entirely different account of the missing VD cattle. He later recounted:

Horn went to Browns Park. Soon after a bunch of twenty-eight head of well bred heifers branded V D belonging to a man in Baggs, Wyoming, were missing. Horn reported that he followed the small tracks of the cattle from the Snake River, east of Beaver Basin. Wiff Wilson and I went back with Horn and were shown parts of the trail. Wilson and I did not go all the way to Beaver Basin. Horns statement had been verified so far, and we instructed him to make an effort to locate the cattle. Horn reported back to the committee that he had found butchered hides bearing the V D brand. One of the hides was found at Jim McKnights summer cow camp at Summit Springs, and one at Mat Rashes N S Camp. Both places were at Beaver Basin. Horn brought the pieces of cowhide for Wilson, Ayers and me to examine. We wet and stretched the hides and found the V D brand on each piece. That looked like the boldest, most outrageous cattle rustling job I had ever seen or heard of. Acting for the general welfare of all range users adjacent to Browns Park, the appointed committee gave Horn the go head signal, and cautioned him to be sure he got the guilty men only.

In retrospect, from Bernard's account of actual events, it seems to lend credence to Ann's assumption that Hicks, alias Horn, was originally involved in the VD cattle appearing in Brown's Park, although Ann had no idea at the time. Shortly after this meeting, Horn, alias Tom Hicks, left the region for a week or two. During this time, in early June 1900, dubious unsigned notices appeared on cabin doors of the Park's more notorious cattle procurers advising them to leave the Park within 30 days or else. The warnings were the subject of local gossip but were largely ignored. Matt and Ann discussed the note they had each received. Ann expressed her concern to her fiancé that she believed it was a threat from Hicks, Rash's former employee. Matt tried to calm Ann by laughing off the matter. Ann was still worried but did calm down somewhat. That is until the July heat of the summer of 1900, when murder shocked the citizens of Brown's Park. Ann later wrote of what was happening at the time with extreme indignation:

> Up to that time nothing had seriously blocked the flood of Two Bar cattle. All obstacles had been successfully removed. Facing failure of the plan, the old Johnson County, Wyoming order for "Extermination" of the obstacle, was put into practice. There was hired secretly one who would strike, kill, and leave no sign. One who would not hesitate to shoot down friend or foe, man, woman or child for pay. In Tom Horn was found this killer, a murderer, lusting for blood money.

On the morning of July 7, Matt rode over to the Bassett ranch to see Ann. After a pleasant afternoon with his fiancé, Matt Rash rode off to his cabin on Cold Spring Mountain. It would be the last time Ann ever saw Matt Rash alive.

Three days later, July 10, 1900, George Rife and 14 year-old Felix Myers, rode over to visit with Matt Rash. As they approached the cabin, an awful smell filled the air. Rash's favorite horse, the gift from Elizabeth Bassett over ten years ago, lay dead near the cabin. A dreadful fear overcame the two as they cautiously approached the cabin. Felix Myers opened the door. Inside, he found the dead body of Matt Rash. The stench was nearly overpowering and flies were everywhere. Myers ran out of the cabin screaming for Rife, who determined the badly decomposed Matt Rash had at least two bullets to his body and had been dead for two or three days. The two rode off to find deputy sheriff Charley Sparks, who rode to the scene of the murder and held an inquest. Sparks and a few other men dug a grave and buried the body of Madison Matthew Rash. The body was so badly decomposed from the July heat that the men covered their mouths and noses with cloths dipped in carbolic acid so as not to breathe in the stench.

It is interesting to note that A. G. Wallihan, owner of the stage station at Lay, Colorado, some 60 miles southeast of Brown's Park, spotted the man known in the area as "Hicks." It was near sundown on July 8, 1900. Wallihan related: "I saw a man on a buckskin horse ride to the top of the ridge and stop and look back. Then he came right down to the crossing, and up the other side. He stopped when he got on top, and looked back again. I recognized him as 'Mr. Hicks.' A day or two after that, I heard that Matt Rash has been killed."

The *Craig Empire* reported the shocking news on their front page:

> Mr. Rash was lying on the bed partially turned over on his face, his head resting on his arm. Two bullet holes were found in his body, one through the back and abdomen, the other in the right breast. On the floor, between the bed and table was a pool of blood which had thoroughly dried. A chair was at the table and the condition of the dishes showed that Rash must have been eating a lunch at the time he was shot. While eating, he was facing a window in the west side of the cabin; behind him was the open door on the east side. Evidently Rash had been shot in the back and when he got up turned around only to be shot again through the right breast. He had fallen where the pool of dried blood was, then revived sufficiently to drag himself to bed.

Rash had one boot off, which peculiarly is accounted for by the fact that he had always removed his boot as soon as he got into the cabin after he had been riding, the foot having been injured some years before and being sensitive, the rubbing of the stirrup caused him some annoyance.

Ann, devastated over the death of her fiancé, knew her suspicions of the stranger, Hicks, were correct. Three days after the murder, Ann paid a visit to deputy sheriff Charley Sparks, explaining her belief that the stranger Hicks, was the murderer. While Sparks was kind to the bereaving Ann, he did not act on her suspicion, even when Hicks returned to the area a few weeks later.

Evidently emboldened by his action and the lack of any investigation from law enforcement, the man known as Hicks let it be known during casual conversations with various folks that Isom Dart may have been the killer, relating the quarrel he had witnessed between Dart and Rash. The gossip was whispered throughout the Park, but nothing came of it; Isom Dart was well known and respected in the area. According to historian John Rolfe Burroughs, "the negro came by most of his cattle honestly." And then, as quick as Hicks returned, he disappeared again.

Meanwhile, Ann and her attorney, Wells B. McClelland of Steamboat Springs, filed a petition at the Routt County courthouse, on August 1, 1900. The "Petition for Letters and Testamentary" was to probate the will of Madison Matthew Rash. Ann claimed that Rash had written a will "on or about the 20th day of May, A. D., 1900," which left his personal property to "his betrothed wife," and "to no one else." However, the petition further stated that Rash had signed the will in front of witnesses, including Elbert Bassett, Josephine Bassett McKnight and E. B. "Longhorn" Thompson. The signed document had been delivered to Ann and that it was in possession "of the petitioner from that time until the death of said decedent; and that since the death of said decedent, your petitioner has searched for the said will and that she cannot find the same." Judge Isaac Voice continued the case, possibly so Ann could find the missing will. Meanwhile, Routt County Sheriff Charles W.

Neiman was appointed administrator of the Rash estate.

At the time of Rash's death, he had approximately 600 head of cattle, mortgaged to the First National Bank of Rock Springs in the amount of 6,000 dollars. The bank's attorney, D. A. Reavill, wrote a letter to Judge Voice contesting the claim of the will and further asked that Charlie Crouse, who was in possession of the cattle, be appointed administrator to the Rash estate. While the judge allowed the bank's interest in the probate case to go forward, he refused to appoint a new administrator.

It was also at this time, in the summer of 1900, that Rash's father, Samuel A. Rash, and one of his brothers, James L. Rash, arrived in Brown's Park, not only to return the body of Matt Rash to his original home in Texas, but also to contest Ann's claim of a will. The Rash family agreed with the bank's position regarding the estate.

After three months of conversing with lawyers and filing legal motions, the case of the estate of Madison Matthew Rash finally received a date in court. Interestingly enough, Ann Bassett rode the long 160-mile trip to Hahn's Peak with Samuel and James Rash. During the trip, the three parties agreed to a settlement. The Rashes offered Ann 250 dollars to settle the case and withdraw her petition. Ann agreed. Arriving at the Routt County courthouse, the parties filed a motion to withdraw Ann's petition. The court judge issued a ruling on the matter on September 24, 1900, which read in part: "The Court after duly considering said motion does order, and adjudge and degree, that said supposed last will and testament so sought to be probated by the said Anna M. Bassett in her said petition is not the last will and testament of the said Madison M. Rash deceased, and that probate is hereby refused."

The final administrators report to close the probate case was filed in court by all parties on October 12, 1900. Sheriff Charles W. Neiman stated that he could account for 485 of Rash's 600 head of cattle.

With the closing of the estate of Matt Rash, it seems as if all parties involved benefited. Sheriff Neiman and his partner, a Steamboat Springs rancher by the name of Horatio Duquette, purchased the Rash cattle from the First National Bank of Rock

Springs, satisfying the bank's interests. Ann Bassett received a monetary settlement of 250 dollars and the small remainder of the estate went to the Rash family, who left Brown's Park with the body of Matt Rash. According to Ann, the Rash family trip back home was delayed. In order to remove the body from the region, the family had to acquire a permanently sealed coffin. Mr. Rash had to travel Rock Springs, Wyoming, to get the coffin and proper certificate for transport of the body. Madison Matthew "Matt" Rash was reburied in the Acton cemetery in Hood County, Texas, in the family plot, near the burial site of his aunt, a sister of Davy Crockett. A large marble stone which marks his burial plot reads:

M. M. Rash
Born
Jan. 4–1865

Murdered in his
cabin on his ranch on
Cold Spring Mt.
Routt County, Colo.

July 8, 1900

A dutiful son,
A faithful friend,
A worthy citizen.

Two months later, in the county election, Neiman was defeated and Joe Jones was elected as the new sheriff of Routt County. Shortly after the election, Sheriff Jones stopped by the Bassett ranch. He was in the Park to serve a bench warrant on one of the citizens in the area. Ann invited the sheriff into the home and to join them for lunch, requesting that he remove his sidearm. Jones complied, laying the gun on the seat next to him. As the group sat down at the table, Jones recognized the man sitting across from him as the man he was after. Ann, with a coffeepot in her left hand, went around the table offering coffee to her guests. When she

Three months after the murder of Matt Rash, Isom Dart was murdered on his property also on Cold Spring Mountain. He was buried there by Brown's Park citizens including Josie Bassett. *Museum of Northwest Colorado*

made her way to the sheriff, while filling his cup, she very carefully lifted his gun from the seat next to him. Setting down the coffeepot, she raised the gun toward Sheriff Jones, while telling the man the sheriff was after to leave. The man did so, mounting his horse and taking the sheriff's horse with him. Ann held the gun on the sheriff for a full 30 minutes, allowing for the man to make his getaway. She then returned the gun to the sheriff and asked him to leave her house. Sheriff Jones left on foot to track his horse. In the end, he found his horse and eventually apprehended the outlaw.

Shock and disbelief rocked the community to its very core when shots rang out again on Cold Spring Mountain. The result was another ghastly murder in Brown's Park.

After the murder of Matt Rash, many single ranchers in the Park sought safety in numbers. Isom Dart was one of those men. With his sizable heard of cattle, he joined in partnership with John Dempshire. The two shared a cabin belonging to Jim McKnight at Summit Spring on Cold Spring Mountain. Throughout that summer, the two men stayed at the cabin but did have visitors. In early October, a few men stopped by to pay a visit. The group included Alec Seger, Griff Yarnell, and the two of the Bassett boys, Sam and George.

Early on the morning of October 3, 1900, the five men and 14 year-old George Bassett left the cabin, heading toward the corral. Suddenly two gunshots rang out in the solitude of the mountain morning. Both of the shots hit Isom Dart, killing him instantly. The five men frantically raced back to the safety of the cabin. The men laid low in the cabin until nightfall, when they made their way out and down the mountain.

After the group reported their harrowing experience and the murder of Isom Dart, several heavily-armed citizens, including Josie Bassett McKnight, traveled on horseback to Cold Spring Mountain. The group found Isom Dart's body, approximately halfway between the cabin and the corral. With a bullet hole to his body and another through his head, Dart was otherwise undisturbed due to the cool fall weather. As a few of the men began digging a burial spot, others surveyed the area for any clues in the murder of their friend. A couple of the men found a spot at the back of the property where a horse had been tied to a tree for a long period. At the base of a large ponderosa pine tree near the edge of the corral, two .30-.30 bullet shells were found. The men were shocked at the discovery. Only one man in the area was known to carry a .30-.30 lever action rifle. That man was the stranger, James Hicks.

After they buried Isom Dart, just west of his cabin in a nice aspen grove, the group solemnly descended the mountain, returning to the community with the news of their discovery. When the Routt County sheriff learned of the murder and the evidence, it was deemed the work of an assassin. Most of the Bassett children had known Isom Dart their entire lives. Josie said of her long-time friend, "[He was] just a good, honest old colored man who never hurt anybody." The *Craig Courier* issue dated October 13, 1900, reported the murder:

Another tragedy occurred in Brown's Park Thursday

morning of last week, Isom Dart, a negro, falling victim to an assassin's bullet. The murder occurred on the Cold Springs ranch. Dart and George Bassett were walking together from the cabin to the corral and when about twenty steps from the cabin door, a shot was fired from the direction of the corral and Isom fell dead. Young Bassett ran back to the cabin, in which were Sam Bassett and Lew Brown, who saw Dart fall when he was shot. The young men were afraid to venture out after the killing and remained in the cabin for four hours. Finally they left the cabin and started for the Matt Rash Ranch. The murderer had stood behind a tree 120 yards from where Dart fell. His tracks where he stood were quite plain and it was evident that the murderer had his horse tied a short distance behind him. The horse was shod and his trail was easy to follow. Sam Bassett and Billy Bragg followed the trail eight miles and when they quit it was perfectly plain.

An inquest was held regarding the murder of Isom Dart, at which time J. S. Hoy also voiced his concerns about the appointment of John Demsher as executor and manager of Dart's estate. At the time of his murder, Dart's assets amounted to a little over 1,000 dollars including personal property and 36 head of cattle. Demsher, who had a half-interest in the cattle, was selected by various citizens and friends of Dart, including Sam Bassett and Henry Hindle. Hoy's concern was that Demsher would move the cattle to Wyoming, which was exactly what he did.

During the murder investigation it was discovered that just the week previous, on September 26, 1900, Hicks filed a complaint at the county courthouse at Hahn's Peak, claiming that Isom Dart had altered the brand on a horse that belonged to Jim McKnight and even named McKnight as a witness.

This claim was ludicrous on a few levels. First, why would McKnight, being a witness to the supposed branding alteration of his own horse not put a stop to it? Secondly, McKnight and Dart were friends. The claim makes no sense. A third point is that at the time the supposed altering of the brand occurred, Jim McKnight

Isom Dart's death certificate. *Museum of Northwest Colorado*

had moved to Utah, having separated from his wife, Ann's sister, Josie Bassett McKnight. Even more incriminating in the sworn claim was that it was signed "Tom Horn." It was the first indication linking the notorious Tom Horn to Brown's Park, but the murder was never proven to be the work of Horn.

An explanation of Horn's filed complaint, specifically naming McKnight, can be offered. Horn had previously shown the evidence of the VD hides to the Snake River Stock Growers Association and had named his suspects: Matt Rash and Jim McKnight. Horn was given the "go ahead" as Bernard put it, to proceed with the murderous task he was hired for, with one caveat: "to be sure he got the guilty men only." With the murder of Isom Dart, who was not a suspect, Horn had to do some quick thinking. In an effort to cover for his mistake, Horn filed the erroneous complaint and in his haste, mistakenly signed his real name. Hiram "Hi" Bernard later said: "Horn made a further investigation and killed Mat Rash and Isam Dart, mistook by Horn, should have been Jim McKnight."

Ann Bassett's long-held belief that Hicks was really Tom Horn, proved to be true. In an indignant tone Ann later wrote:

I believed "Hicks" or Horn, (as he proved to be later)
was guilty of killing both Matt Rash and Isom Dart.
And said plenty but got no support from neighbors and
friends. A letter written by Hicks and mailed to Matt Rash
approximately the same day Rash was killed absolved Hicks
of guilt. In this situation it did not change sound reasoning.
A man could not be in two places many miles apart, on the
same day in those slow times when distance meant days.
The letter caused greater confusion among the people. All
trying to solve a murder mystery and getting no where.

Ann also wrote: "He [Matt Rash] had been shot by
Tom Horn, the stranger he had befriended." The news of the
assassination of Isom Dart sent a chill throughout Brown's Park.
Carl Davidson was 19 years-old that summer. He had spent
most of his summers as a teenager, riding the roundups with the
ranchers of Brown's Park. Davidson later wrote:

> Matt Rash, Isom Dart, and Ed Thomas were earmarked
> for the bounty. Horn tried to stir up a shooting between
> Matt and Isom. I got my information from Charlie Ayers,
> Charlie Crouse and others, George B. Bassett was two years
> younger than I, he was by Isom's side when Isom was shot.
> He was a kid 14 years old. Eb Bassett and Will Davenport
> were in the cabin. I have rode round-up with all of them
> and knew most of the old timers in Brown's Park.

Carl Davidson knew these men well, including Ed Thomas.
Davidson intimately knew of another mysterious murder in the
Park during this time and believed it was also the work of Tom
Horn. He later called the events:

> Ed Thomas was a cowpuncher and had very few if
> any cows of his own. His headquarters was mostly at the
> Bassett ranch in Brown's Park. He left Brown's Park in the
> spring of 1900, went down to Utah.
> There was a man by the name of Walker. I have

forgotten his first name. He had a wife and some kids. I saw him a lot of times around Baggs. He would work at the shearing pins in the spring, then go on to the desert and pull wool–sheepherders didn't skin the dead sheep in those days. When he got through pulling the wool he would work through haying and anything else in the winter.

In the spring of 1899 he pulled out and moved to Rock Springs. Then in the spring of 1900 he disappeared and no trace of him could be found. Some time later, I can't remember the date, his skeleton was found out on the Red Desert. It was identified by a ring he wore. Still, no one knew what happened to him.

In the spring of 1906 I hired out to Charlie Ayers, to ride for him. I had three or four broncs to work out and I got them pretty well broke early in April so he decides to send me to Brown's Park and stay until the Two Bar wagon started work. I packed my bed and took three horses. I went to the L7 winter camp first day. There was a trapper still there; he had wintered there.

There was a big pasture under fence at that time. The fence was all up on the south side of the river and a good size bunch of big steers had come in from the north and crossed the Snake River and they were wanting to get out and head for the mountains. So I decides to clean up the pasture next morning, then visit with the trapper in the afternoon and go on to the Two Bar the next day.

Next morning I rounded up the steers, headed them for the mountains and by that time it was close to noon. I got back to the road coming down the river and pretty soon I heard a commotion behind me and looks around and here is Old Man Ayers working on Keg Head [his horse] with the double end of a hard twist rope.

Well, I thinks, "What the hell now," and know there will be no rest that afternoon. He overhauls me and [says] the Rock Springs Bank is foreclosing on the J. S. Hoy cattle, so the old man thinks he will get some cheap cows.

We get dinner and I pack my bed and we go on

to the Two Bar ranch. Well, on the way the old man gets talkative and he tells me that Tom Horn killed Walker, that Horn mistook Walker for Ed Thomas.

That didn't make sense to me. Ed Thomas was a cowpuncher; Walker was a puller of dead sheep. My version of what really happened was that Horn arrived in Brown's Park too late to get Thomas so Horn sees a man out on the desert alone and shoots him down and claims he killed Thomas and gets the bounty money.

Meanwhile, there was reason to believe that the Bassett boys were also targets of assassin. The October 20, 1900, issue of the *Craig Courier* newspaper reported:

> A report from Brown's Park states that a letter was found among the effects of Isam Dart, the Negro who was recently murdered there, warning the Bassett boys and Joe Davenport to leave the Park inside of 60 days or suffer the same fate which befell Matt Rash and Dart. The boys are interested in ranching and stock in Brown's Park and were raised in that section. They have paid no attention to the warning and continue to attend their interests.

It is interesting to note that Hi Bernard later commented on his involvement of the hiring of Tom Horn. It had long been suspected that Bernard had played a role, but never proven. Bernard finally told the truth to his friend, Francis "Frank" Willis, during the summer of 1917. He had one condition: Willis was not to say anything until after Bernard was dead. Willis agreed. Willis recounted the incident in Bernard's own words in his working memoir, *Confidentially Told*, which was never published. Bernard recalled:

> Haley sent for me to meet him in Denver. I met him there. Haley told me that Wiff Wilson and Charley Ayers were in Denver and had given him a tip on Browns Park conditions. Wilson and Ayers were prominent business and

cattlemen of Baggs, Wyoming. They each had ranches on upper Snake River, and were old timers in the range country of Routt County. A meeting was scheduled for nine o'clock that evening at Hayley's office. We went to dinner and returned to the office an hour or so later. Wiff Wilson, Charley Ayers and John Cobel came in. Cobel was a man of affairs from Wyoming who had extensive range interests north of Cheyenne, and he had been invited to the conference.

The business at hand got under way immediately with Wilson and Ayers bringing up the subject of range in Browns Park. They condemned the place as an outlaw hangout, and a threat to the Haley interests. Both men stated what they knew about the reputation of the Park, and Wilson from personal experience, giving detailed information regarding his losses, he attributed to the thieves of Browns Park and named Mat Rash and Jim McKnight as individuals whom he knew were cattle rustlers. I accepted their word at face value. If the [false] information, regarding Wilsons experience in Browns Park had been passed on to me at the time, as it was four years later, the entire affair might have been quite the reverse of what it was.

Bernard, who was also present at a second meeting of the cattle barons, along with Ora Haley, had this to say of Haley's involvement regarding the hiring of Tom Horn:

Horn was not at the meeting [held in Haley's Denver office,] and Coble acting for him said that Horn was to be paid five hundred dollars for every known cattle thief he killed. Haley was to put up one half of the money. Haley nodded consent to the agreement, but he did not commit himself in words. He instructed me to furnish Horn with accommodations and saddle horses at the Two Bar ranches. After the meeting was over, and Haley and I were by ourselves, he said to me: "Neither you nor I can afford to

133

lay ourselves open to this man Horn. I do not want him on my payroll to kick back and collect money from me in a much more simple manner than by killing men for it."

Perhaps in reflection after so many years, Bernard also said: Horn was not the only one connected with that [murder] affair that should have been hanged. There were several of us that the country could have gotten along without. It always puzzled me why Wiff Wilson and Charley Ayers were over anxious to move in on Browns Park for the kill. Their ranches and range was about one hundred miles from the Park, and they never ranged any stock near the place.

Hiram "Hi" Bernard's evident involvement with the killer for hire, Tom Horn, would be something he would forever live with.

Curiously, and for purely vengeful purposes, Ann Bassett found a way to overlook the deed that ultimately led to the murder of her fiancé Matt Rash. The strong and resilient woman turned her grief over the murder of her fiancé, and the hired hand who taught her how to rope and ride, into a war of vengeance and retribution. Ann began formulating her vendetta against the man, Ora Haley, who had hired the killer, and was attempting to take over beloved Brown's Park.

Tom Horn was later hung for a murder in Wyoming. *Denver Public Library*

CHAPTER NOTES AND SOURCE INFORMATION

For the Burroughs quote on Ann's engagement, see *Where the West Stayed Young*, page 113.

Quotes from Ann in this chapter are found in "Queen Ann of Brown's Park," *Colorado Magazine*, Denver Public Library, Volume XXIX April 1952, and Volume XXX January 1953.

Bernard's quotes are from *Confidentially Told*, the unpublished manuscript by Frank Willis. Willis spent the summer of 1917 with Bernard, caring for cattle near the Green River, west of the Bassett ranch.

Burroughs quote on Hi Bernard and Ora Haley is found on page 76 of *Where the West Stayed Young.*

George Banks' account can be found in the George Banks papers, American Heritage Center, University of Wyoming at Laramie.

Carl Davidson's recollections are found in the archives of the Museum of Northwest Colorado.

While Horn's biographer, Larry D. Ball, says Horn's alias was "Thomas Hicks," local newspaper accounts refer to "James Hicks," as does Brown's Park historian, John Rolfe Burroughs, and Ann Bassett, in her memoirs. Grace McClure refers to both "James Hicks" and "Tom Hicks" in her writings.

Josie's quote regarding Tom Horn can be found in her taped interviews, held at the Dinosaur National Monument, Jensen, Utah. Typewritten account is available at the Museum of Northwest Colorado, Craig, Colorado.

Wallihan quotes are found on pages 208, 214, and 222 of *Where the West Stayed Young.*

The court filings and rulings of Judge Isaac Voice in the probate case of Madison Matthew Rash can be found in the records of the District Court, Ninth Judicial District. Also see Burroughs, *Where the West Stayed Young.*

J. S. Hoy's comments are from his unpublished manuscript, *History of Brown's Park*, 1917.

Carl Davidson's quote can be found on page 211 of Stoddard's, *Tales of the Old West Retold*. It was Sam Bassett, not

Elbert Bassett, who was with the group and Davenport was not among them.

THE VENDETTA

Strong and resilient, despite her grief over the murder of her fiancé, and Isom Dart, the hired hand who taught her how to rope and ride, Ann Bassett launched a personal war of vengeance and retribution. Ann's vendetta was aimed directly toward Ora Haley whom she strongly believed was behind the hiring of Tom Horn who murdered her fiancé. Ann wrote, "we would spot a little bunch of Two Bar cattle down by the river. We forced them into the water. Those that made it to the other side, wandered off into the badlands. In any event, they were lost to the Two Bar, who didn't round up west of the Green."

Ann Bassett had tenacity that seemed to know no bounds. She was not about to lose her beloved ranch or be run out of Brown's Park. Not even when her life was in danger. Ann later told of an unnerving incident at the ranch shortly after the murders of Matt Rash and Isom Dart:

> Three months after the murder of Mat Rash and Isom Dart a man came creeping up to the house on the Bassett ranch...I sat at a table in the living room playing solitaire. Four young boys, Carl Blair, Gail Downing and my brothers George and Eb Bassett, were lunching in the adjoining kitchen. Suddenly the night was shattered by blasts of gunfire. Two bullets came splintering through the door, embedding themselves in the opposite wall, less than six inches from where I had been seated. There could not be the slightest doubt for whom those bullets were intended. I dropped to the floor and rolled under the table. The boys doused the lamp and jumped to a side window, to shoot out into the night in the direction the gunfire had come.

We remained in the darkened house and speculated on why our shepherd dog had not given the alarm of a night prowler's approach; he did not bark all during the night, which was most unusual. That faithful old watch dog never barked again, he had been strangled to death by the spiteful marauder. Fearful of being clipped by shots from ambush, we stayed in the house under cover until eleven o'clock the next day, when two ranchmen, Pete Lowe and Harry Hindle, drove up to the corral in a wagon.

Ann added her own opinion of the escalating violence: "Shadow boxing with bullets is not exactly a glittering adventure anywhere. Not even with our weapons of that day. Our old smoke wagons only let go of one piece of lead at a time. [Before this] it was an accepted practice for each participant to be given an equal start on the trigger squeeze." About this same time, Ann received a notice to vacate the area. Nearly all of the remaining small ranchers in the region had received the same notice. However, Ann's was mailed, not nailed to the door. Ann believed it came from Hicks, the man she believed to be Tom Horn, whom she believed murdered Matt Rash and Isom Dart. Hi Bernard did not

Ann Bassett roamed the range determined to stop Ora Haley's cattle from encroaching on Brown's Park land. *Uintah County Libary, Vernal, Utah*

think the notice or the shooting at the Bassett ranch were the work of Horn. Years later, Bernard told Frank Willis:

> I do not believe that Tom Horn ever fired that shot. It is my opinion that someone from around Baggs got wise to Horn, they did the shooting and left a plain trail on purpose, so the Browns Park people could pick up a clew that would put them on Horn's trail. I have no idea who it was, the [Wiff] Wilson horse that was ridden to Baggs from the L7 Ranch was not ridden by Horn, as reported. The stable man at Baggs claims that he was asleep when the horse was left in the barn. The people in the Park think it was Horn, and proof to the contrary would have been useless.
>
> From what I have heard it did not seem to me that the shot was intended to kill and it could have been fired by anyone of a number of men familiar with the country.

Bernard's statement that the Wilson horse found in the stable at Baggs had not been ridden by Horn, begs a few questions. How did Bernard know that? Did Bernard know more than he told Frank Willis all those years later? And what led him to believe it "was someone from around Baggs"? Did he finally learn why Wilson and Ayers were so interested in Brown's Park, as he had previously questioned? What secrets did Hiram "Hi" Bernard carry to his grave? A defiant Ann Bassett would not be

Ann's nemesis – Cattle Baron Ora Haley.
University of Wyoming

139

threatened. She took the notice to the reporter for the *Denver Post*, who was in the area.

The *Denver Post* newspaper had been covering the events in Brown's Park since the early summer months following the murder of Matt Rash. As the violence and fear escalated, particularly after the murder of Isom Dart, editors at the *Denver Post* sent a reporter to the area to file regular dispatches. One of the first reports included the notice Ann found nailed to her door. The *Denver Post* printed the story, including the fact that unknown gunmen had opened fire on the Bassett family home, in the November 12, 1900, issue:

> Anna Bassett, Lodore, Colo. You are requested to leave that country for parts unknown within thirty days or you will be killed thirty days for your life.
>
> Committee
>
> The note was enclosed in a letter bearing the postmark Cheyenne, Wy., where it was mailed Nov. 15 and has just been made public by Miss Bassett who is now stopping with friends in Craig. Had there been any vigorous effort by the authorities to hunt down the murderer of Rash and Dart the Bassetts would have paid no attention to the warning to leave, but the indifference of the authorities and the presence of suspicious characters in that section led them to believe their lives were in danger, hence all except the father left the country, together with Thompson and Joe Davenport who also had been warned to go by December 12.

The paper followed up with a bold headline in the December 20, 1900, issue:

WAR ON A WOMAN
New Feature to the Routt County Trouble
Outlaws Growing Bolder

They Warn Miss Anna Bassett to Leave The County
Within Thirty Days or Suffer the Consequences

Hayden, Colo., Dec. 20: The latest development in
connection with the reign of terror in central and western
Routt County is the publication of a warning letter to
Miss Anna Bassett who has until recently been living with
her father who is postmaster in Lodore and assisting her
brothers in their ranch and range work.

Several folks in the area left the Park. E. B. "Longhorn"
Thompson, who had a ranch adjoining Haley's Two Bar ranch
on the Snake River, later recounted an altercation with Horn.
Before Horn had a chance to fire a shot, Thompson dove into the
river. Shortly thereafter he moved his family to Vernal, Utah. Joe
Davenport moved to Missouri. Ann's brother, Sam Bassett enlisted
in the army, seeing action in the Philippines. Following his service,
he relocated to Alaska and then moved to Washington. He never
returned to Brown's Park.

It was about this time that Ann purchased property on
Douglas Mountain, known as the Smelter ranch, for 1,500 dollars.
She lived there during the summer months, possibly to escape the

Ora Haley's Two Bar Ranch in Brown's Park. *Museum of Northwest Colorado*

141

Ann's vendetta against Ora Haley included many strategies to reduce the Two Bar cattle holdings, but cattle rustling was never proven to be one of them. *Museum of Northwest Colorado*

violence down in the Park. Ann divided her time between her own ranch and helping out her brothers at the family ranch.

Ann, understandably, was full of rage and resentment over the murders of her fiancé Matt Rash and dear family friend Isom Dart at the hands of a cold-blooded killer she strongly believed was hired by Ora Haley. Now, being threatened to leave her beloved Brown's Park, the only home she had ever known, a defiant Ann fought back. She later wrote: "It was hoped that these methods would 'clean out' and finally dispose of the 'small' outfits, owned by the men and women who had dared intrude on the open public domain, where every American citizen was given a hundred and sixty acres of their own selection to live on." Hell bent on revenge, Ann Bassett boldly stepped up her personal vendetta against the Wyoming cattle baron Ora Haley, and his Two Bar Ranch empire on the western edge of Brown's Park. It would last over a decade.

In her memoirs, Ann wrote:

> I turned the heat against myself by an open declaration
> of war. I rode out of the cedars at the Lew Heard Springs
> and signaled a sour-dough brigade in charge of an army
> of Two Bar dogies en route to Douglas Mountain, and
> informed them what would happen if that herd proceeded
> farther West. It was not an idle threat. I had no support but
> a Winchester rifle with plenty of ammunition, and a place
> picked and fortified. That herd did not go west over the
> divide but were turned forty miles east.

Haley's foreman, Hiram "Hi" Bernard, later said:

> The Browns Parkers did not realize the range was not going
> to be open forever, and they foolishly tried to hold it as a
> private reservation. They knew the Majors and Sainsbury
> ranches on Little Snake River were for sale, and could be
> bought cheap. These ranches were necessary to protect
> their eastern range boundarys, and they failed to buy them.
> That was poor judgment on their part.

Bernard seemed to have Ann Bassett in mind, when he
wrote the following:

> A mere handful of people in Brown's Park set up a little
> kingdom—or queendom—of their own from the Utah and
> Wyoming lines, to the Little Snake River. Except for their
> few ranches, all of it was public land. A big area covered
> with grass and forage, seeding itself and blowing away each
> year, and benefiting nobody. The range used by the big cow
> outfits was not considered private.

Undaunted, and even emboldened by her actions, Ann
continued her efforts to deplete Haley's cattle empire. Ann later
wrote:

143

Throwing caution to the winds, I pushed cattle off the range. I had to work alone. My neighbors did not support me in this, my challenge to Haley, and defiance of law and order. No other stockmen were responsible for what I did. I turned the heat against myself by an open declaration of war.

During one of Ann's illegal episodes, a young teenager, Leath Avvon Chew, was a witness. She later described the incident and her first meeting of Ann Bassett:

On a sunny day in June, I decided to shirk my share of the care of the fat baby Ralph, and go explore a trail that took off from Pot Creek, down a piece. I called Smarty, the little brown mare, slipped on a bridle, and mounted her bareback. I was soon single-footing down a "brand new" trail. The trail led down a gentle incline to a river about one-half mile away, whose banks were thickly lined with cottonwood trees. This I knew was the Green River. Across the river, in the low hills to the east, a dust began to rise. The cause of this was at first hidden. As I watched, a small herd of cattle came into sight and rushed for the river. They were followed by four riders, swinging bullwhips or lariats, whooping and yelling. The cattle rushed into the swift water of the river without slacking pace. They were soon in swimming water. Many were carried downstream a considerable distance before gaining the opposite shore. Greetings were called across river. I impulsively decided to cross. Riding upstream about two hundred yards, I signaled that I was coming over. The game little mare took off into swimming water and I, holding the bridle rein and tuft of the mane in one hand, kept the other hand free for emergencies, floating clear of Smarty's submerged back... We were almost even with those waiting on shore with lassos ready. As the horse touched bottom, I was instantly astride her slippery back. "Crazy stunt" was the greeting. "What's your name?" I felt the attractive young woman was

144

unpleasantly abrupt. I grinned self-consciously as I retorted, "Smarty kin swim and so kin I." Then I said somewhat belligerently, "I am Leath Chew." The woman said, "You are Mark's sister. I am Ann Bassett." I had heard of Ann Bassett. but I did not know then that she was attempting to put into action a plan to destroy all Ora Haley's Two Bar cattle, nor did I know that day of Ann's uncontrollable fear of deep water. The Two Bar spread was on the Little Snake River, and Haley had been credited with trying to get possession of the range in Brown's Park where the Bassett's lived. His method, we were told, was to put two or three hundred head over the divide into Boone Draw, about half way to the Bassett ranch.

Ann also commented on the incident Chew had witnessed: "After that swimming stunt, the cattle disappeared from Brown's Park, not one of them ever straying back." Leath Avvon Chew went on to say of the episode: "This was the beginning of a long friendship between Ann and myself. She was the first woman I ever met whom I both liked and admired." Chew went on to say of Ann's planned vendetta against Ora Haley:

> It was Ann's custom to collect these Two Bar animals and drive them into the Green River, using any help she could get, but generally the young folks with whom she was always a favorite. When crowded into the river, many of the cattle were swept into the canyon by the swift currents, and those that made the west and south bank drifted up Hoy Canyon to Wild Mountain and Diamond Mountain. Without any supervision, they soon fell into the hands of the riders [Ann's helpers], who used the "long rope."

In December 1901, most of the Brown's Park residents gathered at the home of J. S. Hoy for a Christmas dance. Ann Bassett, along with her sister, Josie Bassett McKnight, and younger brother Eb, were in attendance as was Joe and Esther Davenport, Mr. and Mrs. John Jarvie, and several members of the large Chew

145

family. Leath Avvon Chew was 13 at the time and had a teenage crush on Eb Bassett. The younger Bassett boy had just returned from a few years away at college. In her book, *The Chew Bunch in Brown's Park*, Leath Avvon Chew later wrote how excited she was when Eb Bassett put a paper cigar band on her finger. Ann and her "young folks" such as Leath Avvon Chew, who drove off many of the Two Bar cattle, either gave the animals away, or butchered them and gave the meat away in true fashion of Bassett neighborly generosity.

An elderly Leath Avvon Chew. In her youth, Leath often accompanied Ann on her raids of Two Bar cattle. *Uintah County Libary, Vernal, Utah*

Rosalie Miles spent her childhood years in Brown's Park. She later married Ford DeJournette, a successful rancher on the Utah end of the Park. Rosalie later recalled that, as a young girl, her family received some of this fresh beef from Ann Bassett:

> Maybe it was Two Bar beef like they said, but we would have gone hungry without it. They were good to poor people, both Ann and Josie were. We'd be invited to pick apples in the Bassett orchard, and at Christmas they'd be the ones to fix up a tree at the schoolhouse. We wouldn't have had much of a Christmas if Josie and Ann hadn't been there.

Ann seemed to take a liking to many of the young girls in the Park. She would later become close friends with Rosalie Miles.

146

Ann Bassett about the time she met her young vendetta partner,
Leath Avvon Chew. *Uintah County Libary, Vernal, Utah*

However, during this period of Ann's life, she formed a lifelong friendship with Leath Avvon Chew, who would become her partner in crime. Together, the two soon wreaked havoc against the Two Bar cattle outfit. Years later, Avvon Chew Hughel, as she was known, wrote of the many exploits in which the two women were involved in an effort to exact revenge against Ora Haley:

> For hours on end we did nothing but 'jerk' Two Bar steers. Riding full-tilt, we dropped the loops of our lariats over their rumps, flipping them in the air...when they came down, sometimes they broke their necks and sometimes they didn't. Tiring of this, we'd spot a little bunch of Two Bar cattle down by the river. We forced them into the swift current. Maybe they made it across to the opposite bank, but more often they were swept into the mill-race of Lodore canyon and drowned. Those that did make it to the far side, wandered off into the badlands. In either event they were lost to the Two Bar. We were especially active during 1902 and 1903, and we cost Ora Haley hundreds of cattle.

Ora Haley increased the number of hired hands patrolling his ranch land. The men worked in 12-hour shifts, canvassing the area day and night. Investigating the range round the clock, neither Haley's hired hands or the Two Bar's foreman, Hi Bernard, were able to catch Ann Bassett in the act.

In 1903, Tom Horn, having returned to the Coble ranch in Laramie County, Wyoming, went on trial for the murder of 15 year-old Willie Nickell. The jury returned a guilty verdict, which carried the death penalty. On November 20, 1903, the day before his 43rd birthday, Tom Horn was hanged in the heart of downtown Cheyenne, Wyoming.

With the murder conviction and subsequent hanging of Tom Horn, alias James Hicks, the stranger who immediately aroused suspicion for Ann, her long-held belief as to the man's character was confirmed. To Ann, justice had been served for the cold-blooded murder, even if it wasn't justice for her fiancé Matthew "Matt" Rash, and long-time family ranch hand, Isom

Dart. Hi Bernard later commented on the aftermath of Tom Horn's murderous actions in the Park and the reaction of the residents:

> After the arrest of Tom Horn, a hush settled over the range country in Northwestern Colorado, and along the southern border of Wyoming. The big cattle outfits were slowed down. We were skating on thin ice until Horn was out of the way. The Brown's Parkers were on the watch, and waiting to see if another raid was in the make. Ann Bassett grimly rode herd over her favorite hunting ground, making certain that Two Bar cattle did not eat grass west of the Divide.

For awhile, and possibly unbeknownst to Bernard (or maybe he just turned a blind eye), Ann Bassett was doing much more than "grimly riding herd." Through her underhanded scheming, she was putting a sizable dent in the profits of the cattle barons. Almost single-handedly, she soon made the Bassett family a force to be reckoned with in Brown's Park against the large cattle outfits in a way much as her mother had.

Her 66 year-old father, who disliked his daughter's actions as much as he had her mother's, began making extended trips to Los

Rosalie Miles DeJournette always held found memories of her time with Ann Bassett. *Uintah County Libary, Vernal, Utah*

149

Angeles, California. There, he enjoyed the weather and the company of fellow Union soldiers at the local old soldiers' home.

Ann successfully ran the family ranch and fought the cattle barons, particularly, Ora Haley, against a hostile attempt to take over her land. She was a woman in a man's world and she was winning. She not only refused to allow the encroachment of large cattle operations into the area, she refused to share her water rights.

According to Two Bar foreman Hi Bernard, he became aware of Ann's treachery. Bernard later said: "I had never been much of what might be called a 'ladies man' but it seemed the women of Routt County, like side winders, were on my trail. They were chasing me–right out of the country. So I kept mum and kept the Two Bar outfit off the Browns Park range."

Ann took a very bold and calculated step to win her war against Ora Haley. In a tactical turn, she courted and eventually married Haley's foreman, Hiram "Hi" Bernard. Ann explained her reasoning and plan to execute the sabotage of Haley's empire:

> Up to the time of Bernard's buying the Snake River ranches for the Two-Bar, no cattle belonging to that outfit had crossed the divide into Brown's Park. They had not fully stocked the range, and found winter feed near the ranches at Lay Creek. Hi Bernard, whose ability to judge cattle and ranges was perhaps unsurpassed, saw the benefit to be derived by complete control of the entire open range between the Utah line on the west, Wyoming on the north, and east to Hahn's Peak; comprising an area of hundreds of square miles of cow range.

It was an act of spite, as well as for personal and financial gain, when Ann set out to steal away Haley's foreman. Bernard was the most respected and knowledgeable cattleman in the area. She greatly admired Bernard's qualities as a ranchman; no one knew cattle better, and felt he would be able to enhance the holdings of the Bassett family ranch. Hi Bernard later reflected on his first encounter with Ann after she returned from the school in Salt Lake City, in 1895:

150

The following spring I was making a tour of range investigation on the remote Douglas Mountain mesa, and I met Ann Bassett riding alone—a smallish imp of a girl sitting astraddle of a superb horse as though she had grown there. She was dressed in at least one gun. My hands wanted to reach for something high overhead. I restrained them with difficulty, and introduced myself. I got a salty reply that conveyed the idea that gray wolves were natives, and belonged in the country, whereas I was nothing but a Two Bar worm crawling out of the bounds.

For the sake of her ranch as well as relieving her nemesis of his top hand, Ann changed her mind regarding her first thoughts of Hi Bernard. Ann sent a note to Bernard requesting a meeting at her home on Douglas Mountain. Bernard later recounted his thoughts when he received the note from Ann:

> I was not in the mood to put my neck in another loop [for Haley]. Responsibilities kept me around Snake River, and for no reason at all there was a tinge of sentiment in the direction of Brown's Park. I hadn't forgotten that meeting on Douglas Mesa. We are men after all, and when a girl's being savage, she also can be very attractive.
>
> At that time I was thinking seriously of throwing my Colorado job overboard, and trying my luck in Oregon. Then I received a message delivered by Tom Armstrong, an odd character, who was building fence for me west of Snake River. The message was a note from Ann Bassett, requesting me to meet her at the Douglas Ranch. The message both confused and pleased me at the same time. I didn't know what to expect, but I did know that little things like bullets were a minor consideration and would not stop me from trying to reach the ranch. I rounded up my courage and sloped out to keep the appointment.

Thus, Bernard agreed to the meeting with Ann. He later had this to say of the meeting:

When I arrived at Douglas, Ann Bassett was there. Not the stern little guntoter I had seen patrolling the range on Douglas Mesa, but a pretty girl wearing a pretty blue dress that went well with her shining hair. I was invited into the cozy cabin, and told frankly why she sent for me. Ann was contemplating a partnership arrangement to stock the Douglas Ranch with cattle, using the Bassett ranch as a winter base.

Ann, dressed in her most flattering dress, greeted Bernard with all the dainty charm she could muster. During the course of the evening Ann purposed a business relationship between the two whereby Bernard could move his own cattle herd to Douglas Mountain with free use of the ranch land in return for helping Ann and her brothers improve the Bassett cattle ranch. According to Frank Willis, Bernard had a counter proposal. Willis included Bernard's reaction to Ann's suggestion in his unpublished memoirs:

> She outlined the program in a very business-like way and said, "You are a cow man, and if you are interested just think the matter over and advise me of your decision at a future date." As simple as that. By that time cattle and range was the last thing on my mind. When we were called to dinner I had turned to ashes, and I did sure need a bracer of strong coffee to pick me up, for I had a counter offer to make and it needed a lot of backbone that I was unable to locate right then.
>
> So far the most important part of the contract had been overlooked. I did not intend to let that slip away from me. It was not Browns Park and a jumble of sand hills I was after, it was a wife. I braced myself and boldly said so. It seemed the most natural thing in the world for a man to fall in love with a striking young woman and want to marry her. She was not a kid, but was well toward her thirties. She was a capable woman with a mind of her own. She meant something more to me than a toe hold on any country. The woods were full of men, and I was flattered to be chosen

Ann Bassett dressed in her finest to lure Ora Haley's foreman, H. H. Hiram Bernard, away from the Two Bar Ranch. *Museum of Northwest Colorado*

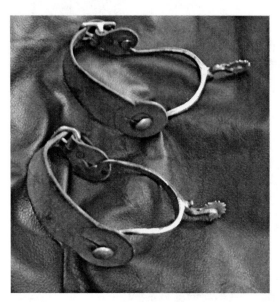

Ann's silver spurs were a gift from her brothers, George and Eb. *Museum of Northwest Colorado*

as her partner. It was strictly cattle with Ann, and she did not pretend otherwise.

Ann agreed to the proposal and the two were married in Craig, Colorado, on April 13, 1904. The bride was 26 years-old and the groom was 46 years-old. It was the first marriage for each of them. The *Craig Courier* carried the news of the marriage in their April 14, 1904, issue:

Yesterday evening, April 13, 1904, at the home of Mr. and Mrs. Frank Ranny, were united in marriage Miss Anna Bassett of Brown's Park and H. H. Bernard. Rev. Anderson officiated during the ceremony. The bride and groom are both well known residents of western Routt County. Miss Bassett's name has been heralded in many parts of the country as a member of the Bassett family of Brown's Park, most of the stories however being imaginative newspaper talk and entirely unauthoritative. Miss Bassett herself is an amiable lady who has many fast friends in her home locality. Of Hi Bernard it is said he is first in one thing at least, and that is management of cattle. Mr. Bernard has no equal in this line in Northwestern Colorado. Every foot of the range is familiar to him, and during roundup season he is king. His qualities in this line are attested by the position of foreman he has held with Mr. Haley for several years. The Courier extends to the new couple most sincere wishes for future welfare and happiness.

Gossip floated among the residents of Brown's Park. How could the woman engaged to Matt Rash, who was murdered by a hired killer paid by cattle barons including Ora Haley, marry his ranch foreman? Even her older sister Josie questioned Ann's judgment. She later said: "When Ann married Hi Bernard, we all objected to that. I never said so to her because she was twenty-three years-old and old enough to know what she was doing. She absolutely didn't. Hi Bernard wasn't on the right tracks. He had helped Tom Horn."

Ann was a complex woman and had her reasons, but she wasn't often prone to explanation to anyone, not even her sister.

Ora Haley was not a man given to gossip. A few days after the couple returned to the

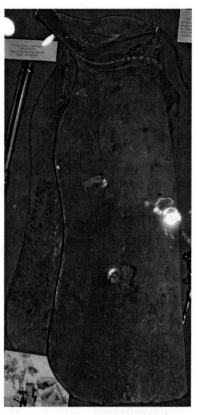

Ann's chaps.
Museum of Northwest Colorado

Park, Haley didn't even bother to meet with Bernard, but sent a telegram, the early 20th century version of a "pink slip"–Hi Bernard was fired from the Two Bar cattle ranch. Neither Ann nor Hi were surprised and Ann was probably thrilled at another victory against the hated Ora Haley.

Bernard had his own opinion regarding the gossip whispered in Brown's Park. He told Frank Willis: "Mountains of hokum has been peddled far and wide about that marriage, made up by nose-ins who were setting up their own standards, and jumping at their own conclusions regarding a private affair."

Despite the gossip swirling around the Park, Hi Bernard settled into married life with Ann as well as any man could with such a perplexing woman. The two were as different as night and day. Hi was calm-mannered and laid-back. Ann was high-strung, manipulative, and prone to impulse. He later remarked of his new in-laws:

> A few of the old pioneers were in Brown's Hole when I came to live here in 1905, Charley Crouse was one of them. He was a regular westerner, enterprising and well liked by all his neighbors, except J. S. Hoy. Another was Uncle Sam Bassett, a grand old man, a bachelor who had made several fortunes in mining at various camps over the West. A miner at heart, and remained a miner to the end of his days.

Despite Josie Bassett McKnight's impression of her sister's new husband, Hi Bernard had the utmost respect for her. He later had this tongue-in-cheek comment regarding his sister-in-law: "Josie Bassett McKnight is a jolly good natured woman, she works like a steam shovel and then she hunts up some unworthy bums and gives away the proceeds of her labor. Her hobby is husbands, she has had five or six good men and discards them one after the other without a backward glance."

Bernard went on to describe his relationship with Ann's brothers:

> Sam Bassett junior became interested in mining in Alaska, he is married and lives there. The most friendly one now living in Browns Park is Eb Bassett. He lives generously, is kind to the human race, and had not dedicated himself to animals. George Bassett's chief concern is in being unconcerned, and he mozies about the business of life in his individual way.

Of his relationship with his father-in-law, Herb Bassett, Bernard had this to say:

> The entire Bassett family is devoted to their father. I never could get acquainted with Mr. Bassett for he is a religious

man, and is away over my head. He peeps over his spects at me and seems to be smiling behind his long white beard as if he was amused by the antics of some strange insect he had come upon by accident.

Following the marriage, Bernard immediately filed for a homestead claim on the east side of Ann's land on Douglas Mountain. He also secured the water rights in the area. With this acquisition, the Bernard-Bassett land encompassed some 1,200 acres where they raised their joint herds of cattle and moved them to the Bassett family ranch for the winter.

Meanwhile, Ann had not relented on her vendetta against Ora Haley. It wasn't enough for her that she had taken his top manager away from him, she continued her vindictive ways of sabotaging Haley's cattle herds whenever she saw the opportunity. If Bernard knew of his wife's actions, he never said.

Approximately a year after the marriage, Ann was hired by the Brown's Park Cattle Association to herd bulls in the Park from the spring calving season throughout that summer. Nine year-old Rosalie Miles never forgot seeing Ann Bassett Bernard for the first time. She later wrote:

> I'll never forget seeing this beautiful woman riding her horse as if molded to the saddle. Thick, reddish-brown hair peeked out from under a large white scarf tied beneath her chin. Her skin was flawless with shining eyes which flashed with fire and life. Her hands were covered with a pair of dainty leather gloves.
>
> Every nine year-old has an idol; this lovely lady of twenty-seven years became mine immediately.
>
> There were no fences in those days, so it was quite a job to keep the bulls from straying away and hunting the cow herd. I immediately decided I wanted to help...and she took a shine to me. I don't know how much help I was, but I enjoyed riding with Ann.
>
> It was always a spectacular sight to watch Ann handle the bullwhip. I remember some of the bulls were

spotted in color. When they started fighting or straying away, Ann could handle that whip and put them in their place.

Ann was married to Hi Bernard at this time. I called him Uncle Hi, and they treated me like a daughter.

Ann had a horse that no one else could ride. Sometimes Ann would wear Uncle Hi's overalls when she rode horseback. Ann loved to wear buckskin britches and so of course I had to have some just like her's.

Ann seemed to have her reasons for riding the way she did. If Ann did get all dressed up like a lady in long skirts, the cowboys would all go into a trance. I rode the same way Ann did, because she told me, "The horses can get kidney sores from all that ridin' on one side."

After a day of herding bulls, we would go back to Ann's cabin. She would always cream her face and take care of her beautiful hair. Loved to listen to her tell stories of the outlaws and the Indians who had roamed in the Park.

By her own estimation, Ann herded over 200 bulls that summer for several ranchers, including her brothers Eb and George. The ranchers paid her a dollar per bull while her brothers paid her with shiny new spurs. In a letter to her friend, Esther Campbell, Ann described her adventurous summer:

> Speaking of a wildcat in Teepee and lower Brown's Draw reminds me of how I became a bull herder. Geo. [her brother George] and Bill Kennon were supposed to have that job. A number of our cattle, some of Sparks, Kennons and Lombards were left or missed on the fall shove off. They were left there two or more years and became pretty wild, so instead of tending bulls at Teepee Geo. and Bill were catching wild cattle. The boys were having a lot of fun—so were the bulls, they were scattered from Lily Park to Cold Springs Mountain. I was not interested in wild cattle so I took over, made a career of it.

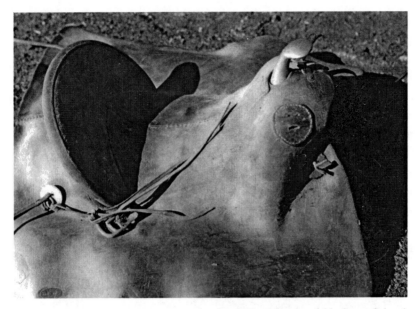

Ann's saddle. *Museum of Northwest Colorado*

This smacks of Ann's wit and a possible tongue-in-cheek account of what she was really up to. It is also possible that by this time, Bernard had an idea what his wife was up to. If so, he never let on. Years later, he said: "Hoy and his tribe of [land] grabbers did not dare to approach Ann on the subject. She hazed the rattle tongues to cover and dealt them to a sizable cussing a time or two, for she understood the situation, and was loyal about it. Loyalty is one of her admirable traits."

The marriage of convenience on the part of Ann was exactly what she wanted. And for the first time, Hi Bernard was raising his own cattle. With Bernard's expertise in ranch management, the Bassett ranch also improved financially. Bernard later commented:

> It was strictly cattle to Ann and she did not pretend otherwise. It was I, who became the unit in a business enterprise exactly the reverse of what you hear today. Together we built up a prosperous cattle business in Browns Park. Ann rode the range with me and that was not the handiest job I ever did. Ann can qualify as an expert in

handling livestock of any kind, and she knows more about cattle than they know about themselves.

Ann's sister, Josie, eventually warmed to her sister's marriage and sent her son, Herbert "Chick" McKnight to the ranch every summer. Ann and Hi both grew very fond of the boy. They understood his wild nature and were patient with him. Hi Bernard had his own manner of discipline, tempered with individual attention and understanding. Bernard treated Chick as a man and expected the same in return. Bernard introduced Chick, at the age of ten, to the cattle experience and Chick was a quick learner. On one occasion, Bernard took Chick to a spot on the Green River where cows often got stuck in the slimy mud. He helped Chick pull the animals free, and let him rescue the calves from the cows that could not be saved. He then gave the dogies to

Chick to raise and care for. A mutual respect formed between the two and for the first time, young Chick respected authority. The Bernards bought Chick clothes, boots, and a saddle. Hi and Chick would often ride horses over to Craig or even north into Rock Springs, Wyoming. The two grew very close. So much so that Hi Bernard would later rewrite his will leaving everything to Chick.

Hiram "Hi" Bernard (far left) is shown with a group of cattlemen at Lakeside Amusement Park in Denver. *Museum of Northwest Colorado*

160

Ann and Hi often took pleasant horse rides together, Bernard on his favorite horse, Old Business, and Ann on her favorite horse, Major, a fine bay gelding, the gift of an early Park pioneer, Joe Reef. It was during one their many rides together, in January 1907 that Bernard spotted a man on horseback riding up and down the opposite side of Vermilion Creek, searching for a place to cross in the icy waters of January. Bernard rode as close as he could to holler at the man and offer help if possible. The man turned out to be Jack Chew, the father of Ann's dear friend, Avvon Chew. Bernard learned Chew was going after the local doctor as his wife had given birth to their 11th child who had died and his wife Mary, Avvon's mother, was suffering due to the difficult birth. Bernard instructed Chew to return to his home, as the rushing creek would subside by morning and he and Ann would cross the creek the next day and do what they could to help the Chew family in their desperate situation. At daybreak the following morning, the Bernards saddled their strongest horses and forged the icy creek. Hi Bernard recounted the harrowing experience:

> We arranged to have several good ropers—among them George and Eb Bassett—stationed on the bank where we were going to attempt a crossing. If a horse failed to swim, or became entangled in the debris and ice, it would be possible for these men to lasso the rider and drag him to safety before he went over the falls. When we were set to take the plunge into the ice-jammed water, I stepped my horse in, and he swam high and easy. Then the cowboys shoved the pack horse into the icy water. By dodging the ice, and swimming strong, he made the landing. Ann came last. Her horse reared, and refused to take the plunge. He was a spirited animal, and when she raked him with her spurs, he made a long jump and went under, and struggled frantically down-stream. Finally, he gained balance and treaded ice, and swam low to my horse on the right bank. The horses were cold and scared. We lit out on a keen run, and kept the pace for a mile. With cold air fanning out our wet clothing, we soon were covered with sheets of ice.

I roped the pack horse and built a fire in a cedar gulch to warm up a little. We put on our dry things and rode up the mountain. The shock of seeing Ann's horse go under water so near the falls almost floored me. That was the first time I realized that I had a bad heart. I damned near died, and thought I could not hold out until we reached the Chew dugout fourteen miles away. I believe the thing that kept me alive that day was Ann riding in the lead with her head thrown back in defiance of all obstacles. On a mission of mercy bent and determined to reach a sick Mother in time to help if needed. We arrived at the Chew Camp about four o'clock in the afternoon, and we found Mrs. Chew very weak and having chills, as she tried feebly to feed her hungry brood. I immediately gathered wood, and soon had a roaring fire. We heated rocks to warm the bed, and gave her a hot whisky toddy.

When Mrs. Chew was made comfortable, Ann pitched in and put the dugout in order, she prepared supper for the children, and put them to bed, then she took the only blanket we had to roll up in, and put it over her saddle horse.

During the river crossing Bernard was scared nearly to death, quite literally. As he watched his wife disappear under the icy water, he suffered from a slight heart attack, yet he persevered and never did tell Ann. He later reflected:

One would not tell Ann that kind of thing. Such an acknowledgment is a mark of weakness to Ann. According to her way of thinking, a full grown man is not supposed to get sick. She takes life on the bounce, and expects a man to do likewise. I still carry in [my] memory that scene of Ann's unbeatable courage in swimming the river and making that long cold ride.

The marriage worked well for a time. The couple even formed their own cattle company. It was Ann's idea, naturally, and

Following the marriage of Ann Bassett and Hiram "Hi" Bernard, the couple lived in this cabin on Douglas Mountain. *Museum of Northwest Colorado*

true to her nature, she had the perfect name: The Bassett-Bernard Cattle Company. To Ann, the name represented the dominance the Bassett family had earned as pioneers of the Park. To Hi, his secondary role in the cattle company, an industry in which he had worked his way to foreman of the largest cattle company in the tri-state region, seemed demeaning. Yet, Ann got what she wanted. She always did. However, the age difference and the fact that Ann was not emotionally invested as was Hi, soon took a toll on the marriage. The two began spending time apart from one another.

Meanwhile, as Ann continued her vendetta against the large cattle companies, she received help from an unexpected source: the United States government. President Theodore Roosevelt, an avid hunter with a particular fondness for Northwestern Colorado, where he had hunted for years, created the Park Range Forest Reserve. Roosevelt signed the Presidential proclamation on June 12, 1905. The Forest Reserve, under the management of the Department of Agriculture, allowed for large acres of land to be used for grazing, for a fee. The cattle barons in the area were furious. Their encroachment of available land had been dramatically reduced.

The largest cattle operations using the Forest Reserve range were the Sevens, owned by the Pierce Rief Company, the Two Circle Bar, owned by the Carey Brothers (John S. and Robert J.), and Ora Haley's Two Bar. Representatives of the Two Circle cooperated with the Forest Reserve officials, while the Two Circle Bar owners, the Carey Brothers, resisted the new regulations for a time. Ora Haley flatly defied the new arrangement. Ann Bassett, who most likely learned the details from Frank Willis, a ranch hand at the time employed by Haley, later wrote:

> The three largest outfits using the range were the Sevens, the Two Circle Bar and the Two Bar owned by Ora Haley. Each presented a different problem to the Forest Service. The Sevens cooperated, the Two Circle Bar offered passive resistance, while Ora Haley presented a front of total opposition. The Two Bar even resorted to stampeding a herd rounded up and ready to count, onto the forest.

The new Forest Supervisor, J. H. "Harry" Ratliff, had a difficult job in dealing with the obstinate cattle barons. Years later, in an interview with Brown's Park historian, John Rolfe Burroughs, Ratliff said:

> It must be remembered that the boundaries of the Forest Service were loosely drawn. They included parts of the intermediate zone where the beef cattle grazed within the forest boundary. It was necessary to know the number of cattle occupying these units of range, which were divided between the reserve lands of the forest, and the unreserved lands remaining as part of the public domain. It was a physical impossibility to control the movement of the cattle without constructing drift fences. It became apparent there was nothing to do but to put the shove up under control, and count the cattle, which is exactly what the larger outfits did not want.

Ora Haley's Two Bar was one of those "larger outfits" that refused to abide by the new cattle counting regulations. Haley had a long-standing dislike for cattle roundups, going back to at least 1896, when he put a public notice in the local newspaper. The *Empire Courier* carried his notice in their May 14, 1896, issue:

Notice to The Public

From and after July 1, 1896 all persons coming to our round-up wagons or ranches for accommodations will be charged 25 cents per meal and 25 cents per day for wrangling horses and hauling bedding for each person. We are always glad to exchange courtesies with our neighboring cattle men, and we only mean fair play adopted by this rule. Our provisions and hay cost us large sums of money, and the cattle business these times don't justify free grub and hay to the extent now imposed on us. It has been the custom of certain parties to take up and ride horses belonging to our outfit and also drive our bulls off the range to run their cattle. Hereafter, in no case will any person not in our employ be allowed such privileges without authority from the undersigned or their respective foremen.

Ora Haley

In the summer of 1909, Haley expanded his cattle operation with a little help from Ann's other enemies:; the Hoy brothers. On June 18, 1909, J. S. Hoy and his brothers sold a portion of their land to the Haley Live Stock and Trading Company. A large bunk house was built on this land to accommodate Haley's added employees. With the increase in manpower, Haley presented a front of determined resistance and open defiance. It would be his first public defeat in his desired land acquisition scheme. Ann, in her memoirs, described how the new situation affected the operations of the cattle barons:

The Two Bar outfit, under range management of Bill Patten considering themselves rolling juggernauts, refused to pay the negligible grazing fee requested by the United States forest department. They could not bribe the forester, nor deceive him by false counts of cattle, so they attempted to slay the regulations of control set up by the government order, thereby forcing the forester, to count all cattle grazing on the National Reserve. This act of counting the cattle was resented by Ora Haley, who flatly refused assistance to the forest department. Progress of the necessary round-up, was retarded by every imaginable means. The foreman on the range scattered cattle over wide areas adjacent to the forest, knowing they would drift into the reserve from many places. There were no fences to protect this National Reserve, and the rounding up, holding and counting of so many thousand of cattle on an open range, is an undertaking of colossal proportion.

Under the direction of Ora Haley, the Two Bar foreman, Bill Patton, ordered his hired hands to actually force a stampede of the cattle after they had been rounded up and were ready to count. Ann later recounted the event:

> The rounding up had been accomplished by much grilling labor, and a great expense, by the Forest Department. The Two Bar foreman, Bill Patten, had persistently kept up a moving row in a long range effort to over-run the beef cow country In parts of three states, to keep it free and open for the Two Bar, and nobody else. When twenty-five thousand cattle were being held on the bed ground the last night before they were to be counted and turned on the Forest Reserve, he left the roundup camp giving a flim-flam excuse. He slunk back at midnight with a few rocks in a tin can to toss at an alert old cow and snap her into action. And he carefully timed his movements when the night guard was trotting around in the other direction.

What did Patten care for a few mangled and dead cowboys, or for cattle killed and crippled by the run of a herd of that size in a head-on rampage, as they rushed over rocks and heavy, down timber. Some of the Two Bar's [cattle] would escape and get into the reserve uncounted.

It would teach the stubborn Forest Supervisor, Harry Ratliff, a lesson, providing he survived the death race of the stampeded cattle.

Ann was correct in her assessment of the situation. Ratliff and his rangers had set up camp, near where the cowboys were watching over the concentrated herd of cattle. When the tin can full of rocks was tossed by Patton, it resulted in the desired effect. The startled cattle ran, soon causing a stampede. Fortunately, the stampeding cattle ran in the opposite direction of the camp and no one was injured by the derelict action.

Ann believed that Patton caused the stampede to scare Ratliff and the Forest Service authorities, with the hope that it would put an end to the government imposed roundups that Ora Haley resented. In fact the act by the Two Bar foreman had the opposite effect. Ann continued with her account:

Ann Bassett roping cattle at the family ranch. *Uintah County Libary, Vernal, Utah*

The cowboys gathered on high ground in grey morning to roll Bull Durham cigarettes and decide what was to be done about attempting a new start, to round up the cattle. They found that Ratliff and his rangers were right there with them. The 'tender feet' Government employees were boys that could take it rough, and they had the intelligence to map out a course to handle the situation.

Harry Ratliff called into counsel the Seven and Two Circle Bar men and had cowboys stationed along the forest boundary to keep any cattle from crossing the line. Other riders made a sweeping circle and bunched the cattle near the line to be counted across by the Forest Rangers. The Two Bar riders continued to pass up cattle that should have been driven to the bunch ground. That was stopped when a Seven or a Two Circle Bar cowboy rode circle with each Two Bar man. Very few of those cattle entered the Forest Reserve without being tallied by the rangers. The effective manner in which the work was carried out was a big surprise to the Two Bar foreman, Patten.

Patten went to Ratliff and threatened disastrous counterblasts if he insisted upon interfering in the Two Bar's range affairs. At that point in the argument Patten found that he had made a serious mistake. Ratliff did not become frightened and run away, he called Patten's hand. He sternly dished out a program that left Patten speechless, white with fury.

Patten had taken too many things for granted. If he had informed himself about the background of Ratliff and his assistants he would have learned that they were frontier bred and born, that they had been handling cattle on the range when he was hoeing cotton on a farm in North Carolina.

He could see how he was being outmaneuvered and he changed his tactics.

Little did Ann know that Bill Patton's "change in tactics" was aimed straight at her. It was just a matter of time.

Meanwhile, Ann was dealing with domestic issues. During the winter of 1909-1910, Hi left the Park for several months on a business trip to Denver. Ann elected to stay behind, possibly because she was the Census taker for the Brown's Park region. Interestingly enough, this was also the first winter she stayed at the Douglas Mountain ranch, rather than winter at the lower elevation of the Bassett family ranch.

A handful of unemployed ranch hands, including a young cowpuncher by the name of Tom Yarberry, ventured over to Douglas Mountain and eventually to Ann and Hi's ranch. Ann took them in for the winter, as well as a woman, Mrs. Hurd, and a man known as J. K. Klinger. This gesture on Ann's part was purely second nature. She had grown up in a home where her parents often took in friends as well as strangers. It was a Brown's Park neighborly custom started by Elizabeth Bassett all those years ago.

When Bernard returned to Brown's Park in the spring of 1910, he was furious that so many strangers were now living in his home. Pitching a tent, he chose to stay outside of the home and whatever Ann had going on. One night the loud noise from inside the log cabin was too much for Bernard. He fired his rifle into the air. That fired shot put an end to the marriage.

The once agreeable couple again agreed, perhaps for the last time, on a divorce. It would be nearly three years before a petition of divorce would be filed in the newly created Moffat County. This was possibly due to separating the couple's finances and the fact that Ann was Catholic. While Ann was dealing with the end of her marriage, her new nemesis, Haley's ranch foreman, William "Bill" Patton, was devising a plan to bring her down.

CHAPTER NOTES AND SOURCE INFORMATION

Ann Bassett Willis wrote of her life experiences in a four-part series published in the Colorado Historical Society's *Colorado Magazine*. The series, titled, "Queen Ann of Brown's Park," ran in Volume XXIX January 1952, Volume XXIX April 1952, Volume XXIX October 1952, Volume XXX January 1953. They are available at the Denver Public Library. Unless otherwise noted, the quotes attributed to Ann are from this work.

Hiram "Hi" Bernard's quotes are from *Confidentially Told*, the unpublished manuscript by Frank Willis. Willis spent the summer of 1917 with Bernard, caring for cattle near the Green River, west of the Bassett ranch.

Leath Avvon Chew quotes come from *The Chew Bunch in Brown's Park*, by Leath Avvon Chew Hughel.

Rosalie Miles DeJournette's quotes are in the DeJournette family files. Also see DeJournette, Dick and Daun, *One Hundred Years of Brown's Park and Diamond Mountain*, pg. 225.

Josie's quote regarding Ann's marriage to Hiram "Hi" Bernard can be found in her taped interviews, held at the Dinosaur National Monument, Jensen, Utah. Typewritten account is available at the Museum of Northwest Colorado, Craig, Colorado.

Ann's letter to Esther Campbell can be found on page 94 of *The Bassett Women.*

Harry Ratliff's interview can be found on page 293 of *Where the West Stayed Young.*

The records of the sale of Hoy land to the Haley Live Stock and Trading Company can be found at the Museum of Northwest Colorado, Craig, Colorado. It should be noted that the record includes the name of Valentine S. Hoy. This is incorrect; he was murdered by the outlaws Harry Tracy and David Lant, in 1898.

Moffat County was formed from the extreme western portion of Routt County, including Brown's Park, by the Colorado State Legislature in 1912.

QUEEN ANN

Ann remained at her cabin on Douglas Mountain, running what remained of the Bassett-Bernard Cattle Company. Continuing her vindictive actions against the large cattle barons and, particularly, her nemesis Ora Haley, Ann denied access to her water on Douglas Mountain to any Two Bar rancher and their cattle.

Following some legal trouble, J. S. Hoy had sold his ranch to Ora Haley in 1909. Despite this acquisition, the Two Bar ranch suffered financially after Haley fired Hi Bernard. A few unsuccessful replacements only made matters worse for Haley and his operations. Perhaps Ann thought she was finally gaining an upper hand on her nemesis. When Haley hired 40-year-old William "Bill" Patton as manager of the Two Bar, Ann's war against Haley took a decided change in direction. When Patton was told that Ann Bassett Bernard was denying Two Bar cattle access to water, he put a plan of entrapment in motion.

On March 15, 1911, a weather-beaten prospector who introduced himself simply as "Mr. Nelson," showed up at Ann's Douglas Mountain ranch. Ann, as was her neighborly custom, let the man sleep in the barn. The following morning Nelson left the ranch, presumably to prospect in the hills near the area. In reality, this "Mr. Nelson" was a stock detective in the employ of the Two Bar ranch, hired by Bill Patton. The objective was finally to put an end to Ann's vindictive acts against the Two Bar. Nelson was charged with finding evidence of cattle rustling by Ann and whoever else he could.

Three days later, Nelson rode to the Two Bar ranch and reported to Patton that although he had not witnessed the butchering, there were three quarters of a fresh beef hanging in the

171

meat house on Ann's property. He also reported seeing a pair of
women's shoes with blood spots on the back porch of Ann's home.
The two men headed back to Douglas Mountain, making camp for
the night a mile from the ranch.

The next morning they set out to retrieve what evidence
they could. Why Nelson had not at least secured the evidence
in a proper manner for the authorities to investigate is unclear.

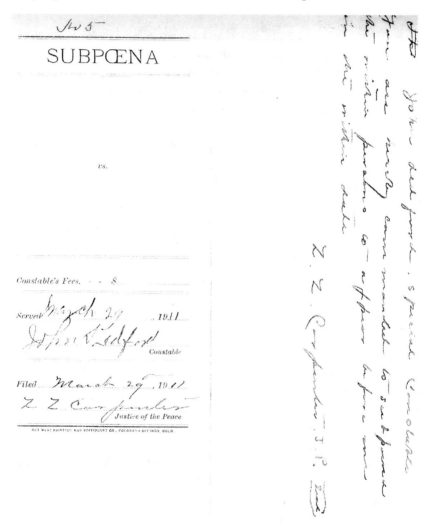

Judge Z. Z. Carpenter's handwritten subpoena for the arrest of Ann Bassett.
Museum of Northwest Colorado

Allegedly, as it would later become a point of contention at trial, the following morning the men found the hide of a recently butchered heifer. Patton hid the hide among the brush. Then the men left to notify Sheriff Ledford, and swore out a complaint of cattle theft against Anna M. Bassett Bernard and Tom Yarberry, who acted as ranch foreman after Hi Bernard left the ranch.

Ann, of course, was outraged at the accusation. Being accused of cattle theft was a serious charge, something that not only Ann, but her fellow ranchers, deeply resented. It was common knowledge throughout the Park of her vendetta against Ora Haley and the Two Bar cattle ranch. While many of the smaller ranch owners agreed with her, none of them participated in her cause. Yet as time went on, nearly all of those ranchers agreed that Haley and his strong-arm tactics were hurting their own cattle operations. As Ann herself later said, she was becoming "setfast on the withers of the Two Bar." Ann later offered her observations of the event that led to her arrest of cattle theft:

> Range invasion was stubbornly resisted by the Brown's Parkers and consequently; we were attacked from every angle. Rumors were circulated to the effect that not only were we cattle thieves ourselves, but we harbored outlaws and criminals from other states; that in general the park was a refuge for no-accounts to carry on their cussedness. It was the old game of giving a dog a bad name and then go gunning for him, a method strictly in line with the mean practices followed by some of the big cattle organizations. Not all cattle owners of the large scale were of that stripe. By their true quality and principle they prospered and made money, while the Two Bar and its various managers went down and out. This Two Bar outfit has been charged with and is probably guilty of every crime from murder to sheep killings. They contributed practically nothing to the support of the counties their enormous outfit took over.

It is also interesting to note that Patton was under pressure to improve the bottom line of the Two Bar. He was known as a ruthless man, with a shady past, rumored to have participated in a little cattle brand alteration of his own, as well as rustling his own fair share of cattle. The ranchers of Brown's Park who had respect for his predecessor, H. "Hi" Bernard, had no respect for this man. Ann later had this to say about Bill Patton:

> The way Patton handled the Two bar cattle was brutal and uncalled for. For his riders drove them at a trot, punished and beat them along the trails, and shoved them miles beyond their beyond their strength. He rushed the herds on, and scattered them widely for the sole purpose of grabbing [smaller] holdings, and destroying the range and forcing the settlers and owners of small herds to move out or starve out. Patton was a range ravisher.

Perhaps in an attempt to prove his worth to Ora Haley, Patton rushed forward with the cattle theft charge against Ann Bassett. On March 29, 1911, Justice of the Peace, Z. Z. Carpenter issued a subpoena for Anna M. Bassett to appear before him. In the margin of the subpoena Carpenter hand wrote the following: "John—you are hereby commanded to subpoena the within persons to appear before me in the within date. Z. Z. Carpenter. J. P."

"John" was Constable John D. Ledford who served the subpoena to Ann. Two days later, March 31, 1911, Ann dutifully appeared before Z. Z. Carpenter. Following the hearing, Carpenter ruled that Anna M. Bassett be held on charges of cattle rustling. Bond was set at 1,000 dollars, which she was easily able to provide. Defiant, not to mention enraged, Ann later wrote of the experience: "The curtain was up and the show about to begin. There in solemn pomp and owlish dignity sat the judge on an upturned dry goods box, looking like an ancient museum piece, and knowing about as much law as the box he sat on." Following the preliminary hearing, Ann learned the esteemed attorney, A. M. Gooding of Steamboat Springs, was in Craig, Colorado, representing another party in a cattle rustling case. She made the trip to Craig and met with Gooding. After hearing Ann's version of the charge against her, the attorney had no desire to take the case.

However, perhaps in an effort to save himself from turning down the genteel lady sitting across from him, he set an enormous fee of 1,000 dollars, in advance, believing she would turn him down and seek other council. The charismatic Ann didn't bat an eye as she leaned down and pulled out a roll of cash from her stocking. She then peeled off ten 100 dollar bills and, with a smile, handed them to the attorney.

The preliminary hearing in the case of "The State of Colorado versus Ann Bassett and Thomas Yarberry" was held in the District Courthouse in Craig, Colorado. The account in the *Craig Empire* newspaper, dated April 1, 1911, set up the events and all the sensational aspects that would hold the attention of Brown's Park and Craig citizens for months to come.

> The case attracted widespread attention, and people came from miles around to be present at the hearing. Ora Haley, owner of the Two Bar came from Laramie, and Jerry Pierce, another of Northwestern Colorado's biggest cattle raisers, arrived from Denver. Hi Bernard, who had been in Denver for several months, got here with all possible speed to be with his wife in her time of trouble. Craig citizens 'chipped in' and rented the opera house so that all might have an opportunity to hear the evidence. W. B. Wiley, attorney for the Cattleman's Association, was in Steamboat Springs, prosecuting another alleged female rustler the fore part of the week, so the preliminary hearing was set for Thursday. A. M. Gooding of Steamboat Springs, appeared for the defendants. The case was commenced before Justice Z. Z. Carpenter in the forenoon, and adjourned to 2:30 in order to give some of the prosecuting witnesses time to get here. It was not necessary to wait, however, as no testimony was taken. At the afternoon session, the defense took a change of venue to Justice D. C. Crowell. When things were again ready for business, and the defendants waived examination, Judge Crowell fixed their bond at one thousand dollars each, and the case was closed until district court next August.

The *Craig Empire* newspaper continued its reporting with a bit of sensationalism that would forever remain with Ann Bassett:

> Interest naturally centered in Mrs. Bernard, who is really a remarkable personage. Raised in the wilds of Northwestern Colorado, trained from childhood to ride and shoot, she has a splendid education which has been improved by extensive travel. She is said to be as much as at home at a swell social function as while taking her regular "watch" with the other cowpunchers on the roundup. As she appeared in court Thursday, stylishly attired, she looked the part of "Queen Ann" with her wealth of brown hair and stately carriage.

With the *Craig Empire* first using the moniker of "Queen Ann" it soon became the standard in newspapers across the country covering the sensational trial. It would become a "badge of honor" to Ann and a term used by historians to this day. Ann's long time friend, Esther Campbell later wrote. "The name 'Queen Ann' fit her to a T. She didn't want to be anyone else." However, Ann's sister Josie, had a decidedly different perspective. Josie later commented:

> Well, she [Ann] is to blame for all that 'Queen Ann' stuff herself, 'cause Ann had a terrible temper, uncontrollable temper. There was a writer out one time. Oh, I don't know what he was for, he followed her around everywhere. He was asking Ann too many questions that she didn't want to answer, so she said 'its none of your business, now you go away and leave me alone, its none of your business.' So he gave her that 'Queen Ann' business and that's where that started, from her own high tempered stuff, and it stayed with her as long as she lived.

The trial of "The People versus Ann Bassett Bernard and Thomas Yarberry" began in August 1911, with District Court Judge John R. Shumate presiding. The lead prosecuting attorney was District Attorney James Gentry. He was assisted, interestingly

This building in Craig, Colorado, served as the courthouse until 1925. Both cattle rustling trials against Ann Bassett were held in this building.
Museum of Northwest Colorado

enough, by W. B. Wiley, an attorney for the Stock Association. For the defense, A. M. Gooding Sr. enlisted the help of Colorado's top criminal defense attorney, Miles G. Saunders of Pueblo. The trial lasted less than a week and resulted in a hung jury. The Saturday, August 12, 1911, issue of the *Craig Empire* reported the trial events in great detail:

> Great care was exercised by the attorneys on both sides in the selection of the jurymen. The original jury list of thirty-six was soon exhausted, eighteen were drawn on special venire Wednesday morning. Shortly after the noon recess, a jury was selected and sworn in. At all times during the trial, the courtroom was packed to suffocation, and, although there was little of a startling nature in the testimony, the spectators thoroughly enjoyed the legal battle of the opposing attorneys.

The prosecution presented the facts of their case: that a cow had been butchered and the fresh meat found hanging in the meat house on Ann Bassett Bernard's property. Witnesses to finding the butchered beef were Nelson and Bill Patton of the Two Bar. Billy Wear of the Sevens ranch and the hated Ora Haley were also witnesses for the prosecution. In their opening statement, the defense council conceded to the evidence found at Ann's ranch. However, defense attorney Saunders claimed he would establish beyond a reasonable doubt that the butchered animal did not belong to the Two Bar Cattle Company.

As the prosecution presented their case and called witnesses, Saunders cross-examined Bill Patton regarding the cowhide he and Nelson discovered. When asked how he knew the hide belonged to the Two Bar, Patton stated that "someone" had cut away the right flank of the hide in an effort to get rid of the brand. Patton went on to testify that he could still determine the hide as one of Haley's animals by the way it had been spayed. Ann's brother Elbert "Eb" was called to the stand by the defense. Asked who and why someone would remove a portion of the hide but leave the rest intact to be found, Bassett simply replied, "someone who would want to frame my sister." The *Craig Empire* continued their coverage of the trial:

> Ebb Bassett a brother of Mrs. Bernard, testified that he went to the Bernard home alone about noon on March 13th, and being informed by his sister that she was about out of fresh meat, he told Tom Yarberry to bring in the heifer they had been saving to butcher. Yarberry did so, Bassett shot the animal, and the two removed the hide and entrails, which were left on the spot. He said he had used the 7 L brand about seven years, but never had it recorded. Mrs. Bernard, who said she had been a resident of this county for thirty-two years, and that her present ranch about seven years, gave like testimony regarding the beef in the controversy. Her ranch had been a common watering place of cowmen until she forbade them in

December 1910. H. H. Bernard, husband of the defendant, and for ten years foreman for the Two Bar, said that he had spayed probably two thousand heifers for Haley, that it would be impossible to distinguish a spay mark from scars caused by other wounds after two or three years. On Friday morning, Hi Bernard was recalled to testify further regarding the mark on the hide introduced in evidence by the prosecution, he having made an examination in the meantime. Chick Bowen swore that, while riding in from Lay with Foreman Patton, a day or two before the arrest, Patton had told him that Mrs. Bernard was in the way, and that he would get rid of Yarberry, even if he had to put up a job on him. Emery Clark, who was with the Two Bar roundup wagon in September, 1910, stated that Patton, in referring to Mrs. Bernard and Tom Yarberry, had said that he wanted to "get rid of those two s.o.bs." Mrs. Bernard was recalled. Attorney Saunders asked: "Did you or did you not, on or about the 15th day of March, 1911, appropriate, steal, drive away or kill a heifer belonging to the Haley Livestock and Trading Company, and bearing the Two Bar brand on the right hip?" In a clear, firm tone the defendant [Ann] replied: "I did not; nor at any other time."

After closing arguments and jury instructions, the jury retired for deliberation. The following day, the jury foreman reported to the judge that an agreement regarding a verdict was impossible. Thus, with a hung jury, a new trial would be scheduled and Ann Bassett Bernard would have to fight the cattle baron, Ora Haley, once again. The *Craig Empire* reported the conclusion of Ann's first trial: "...the jury reported this morning at 10:30 that an agreement was impossible. Consequently Judge Shumate discharged the twelve men, and the case will be on the docket at the next term of court in the county, February, 1912."

J. S. Hoy later commented on the trial:

This photo of Ora Haley in the center, taken in Craig, Colorado, may have been during the time of the cattle rustling trials. *Museum of Northwest Colorado*

When the defense opened its case, Attorney Saunders stated that the discovery of fresh beef in the Bernard home by Detective Nelson and others was admitted, as well as the finding of the hide and offal. He admitted that Thomas Yarbery and Ed Bassett, a brother of Mrs. Bernard's were present. The defense would show, the attorney said, that the animal in question was not the property of the Haley Livestock and Trading Company, but was owned by Ed Bassett, branded 7L on the right side, and that it had been on the Bernard premises for months prior to the killing. The testimony of Mrs. Bernard, Ed Bassett, Matthew Morelock and Eugene Malon, all of whom were present on March 13th, when the animal was killed, was in line with this statement, and all swore that they did not mutilate the hide as was charged by the prosecution.

Two witnesses were introduced to refute the testimony given by W. M. Patton, foreman of the Two-Bar, who stated that there was no desire on the part of cattlemen to run the Bassetts out of the country, and denied that they had ever made threats. "Chick" Bowen, a cowpuncher, swore that Patton told him that the cattlemen needed the water at Douglas Springs, as the real reason for the arrest of Ann. The prosecution failed to show by witnesses that Haley's Two Bar Ranch was the only outfit whose cattle were branded on the right side. One witness, Alesworth, who lived just across the state line in Wyoming, testified that he owned cattle branded on the right side, and that the hide found at the Bernard Ranch might have at one time, covered one of his steers.

Ora Haley, complaining witness and owner of the Haley Livestock Company, claims to have lost other cattle through Mrs. Bernard and Yarberry. Ora Haley took the stand, but when pinned down by counsel for the defense, could not make any positive statements. This closed the first trial of Ann, the jury failing to agree on a verdict.

The citizens of Craig cheered as Ann left the court proceedings. She had won this round and gained many supporters. Historian John Rolfe Burroughs wrote: "Spiritually as well as physically, she was as tough as rawhide and as resilient as rubber. And yet when she so desired she could be the personification of fragile femininity."

On the other hand, hatred for Ora Haley only grew more intense for many citizens throughout northwestern Colorado. The second trial was postponed due to a series of unforeseen events. A few of the defense witnesses had left the area. Tom Yarberry had skipped bail and also left the area. Eb Bassett, who had put up his bail, was left to settle the debt with the court. Ann was in El Paso, Texas, supposedly recovering from a severe illness, as the press reported. She had alerted her attorney, who filed a motion with the court for postponement.

Another defense witness, Chick Bowen, well thought of throughout the region and one of the more important witnesses for the defense, had been shot and killed in Baggs, Wyoming, in

January 1913, by deputy sheriff Bob Meldrum. Meldrum had worked with Tom Horn in catching rustlers in the Wyoming area and was rumored to have aided Horn in his exit from Brown's Park after the murders of Matt Rash and Isom Dart. A few years later, the large cattle barons, including Ora Haley, backed Meldrum and even provided money to have Meldrum appointed as deputy sheriff of Routt County. The citizens flatly refused the obvious attempt to make an associate and co-conspirator (after the fact) of a paid killer as a deputy sheriff. The *Steamboat Pilot* newspaper, which generally supported the cattle barons interests, ran the following editorial in the December 8, 1908, issue: "This paper will oppose to the last ditch the giving of any professional man-hunter a sheriff's deputyship, or anything else which would give him a badge of authority for shooting down any of Routt County's citizens."

Meldrum did not get the appointment and moved to Baggs, Wyoming, where he did receive the appointment as deputy sheriff. Incredibly, Carbon County Wyoming Sheriff Horton defended his hiring of Meldrum by offering this explanation to the Steamboat Pilot, printed in the December 16, 1908, issue: "I have been greatly criticized for calling upon Meldrum...Many people do not like Meldrum's methods, but I can't help that. Nearly all the cattlemen are behind him, and will stay with him, no matter what he does."

The *Craig Empire* delivered the shattering news of the murder of Chick Bowen in the January 26, 1913, issue:

As Bowen was leaving the hotel after supper, Meldrum told him he was under arrest for yelling while crossing a bridge on the way home ten days before. All except the marshall considered it a joke at first, but when Bowen's hat blew off and he attempted to recover it Meldrum commenced shooting. The first shot entered Bowen's left leg while the second struck the top button of his overalls and glanced off.

At this stage of the game the cowboy realized that Meldrum was in earnest and proceeded to use nature's weapon on the bad man. With his fists he broke the officer's nose and pummeled him until he yelled for mercy. Deputy Sheriff James Davis pulled Bowen off and as he did so Meldrum fired again, the shot taking effect in the groin. Ann later wrote of the murder of Chick Bowen:

> Chick was not the sucker type nor a blow-off kind. He could not be bought off by the Meldrum gang, consequently he was listed as being dangerous to their interests. He moved to Baggs and went to cowpunching for the Salsbury boys, two young men favorable to range control by the Forest Service. Chick was a jolly, friendly boy with a sense of humor. Riding into town one day, he met a friend, and as they were standing on the sidewalk he laughed at some joke that passed between them. Meldrum rushed up to Chick and charged him with creating a disturbance. The words were scarcely out of his mouth when he shot three bullets squarely into Chick's body, killing him almost in the instant.

Evidently, Ann was well aware of Bob Meldrum and his reputation. She later recalled an incident involving Forest Supervisor Harry Ratliff and Bob Meldrum. This occurred shortly after Bill Patton, foreman for Haley's Two Bar outfit, had caused the stampede of cattle at the roundup in the summer of 1909, on the National Forest Reserve land:

> Baggs is located on the Colorado-Wyoming state line and is also near the National Forest Boundary where surveying was in progress. All of the stockmen in the district were vitally interested in the success or failure of the Routt National Forest Reserve.
> If the Forest Department gained control there would be supervised grazing on the summer range, and sheep permits issued. The cattlemen had kept the sheep off the range by force. Large piles of bleaching bones of sheep in different places were mute evidence of the ruthless method

in practice to hold the range, exclusively for themselves. Forest control meant regulations in the number of livestock permitted to graze within the boundaries.

When Ratliff arrived in Baggs he was met by his chief assistant, Chas. Morell, who informed him that Bob Meldrum, notorious gunman, had come to Baggs and was appointed Town Marshal.

Survey work was going ahead rapidly with Ratliff in charge. He was sighting through his telescope when a when a gunshot exploded from ambush and his transit fell to the ground. One leg of the tripod had been shot away. He armed himself and his helpers and continued surveying. Toward evening Ratliff and Morell took their pack horses to Baggs for supplies. They were leading their horses into the livery barn when town marshal Meldrum approached and demanded their guns. They refused to give them up to him. Medrum made a move for his shoulder holster, but before he could draw he was looking into the muzzle of a Colts forty-five held by Ratliff. This unexpected move completely nonplused the marshal, his killer instinct vanished for the moment. Meldrum stared dazedly as Ratliff removed the gun from its holster, shoved it under the waist band of his own pants, and walked away. That was Meldrum's last attempt to intimidate the foresters.

When news of the shooting death of Chick Bowen at the hands of Meldrum reached northwestern Colorado, the citizens were outraged. The fact that the sheriff of a Wyoming county would hire such a man as Meldrum, who represented the cattle baron's interests and who later killed an innocent, respected man of the region, remained in the minds of most of the citizens of Northwestern Colorado. The memory of Chick Bowen's murder lingered in the minds of these people when Ann Bassett's court date neared and potential jurors were eventually summoned.

Finally, the District Court session was scheduled. It would be the first in Moffat County since the creation of the new county, with Craig as county seat, the previous year. The *Craig Empire* carried the story in the August 10, 1913, issue:

An extra large docket of civil and criminal cases awaits Judge Shumate's decision in the first Moffat County Court.

District court convenes here next Tuesday, August 13, with Judge Shumate on the bench. A great many civil and criminal cases will come up for trial this term, because no court was held last February and many were postponed. The criminal cases are not definitely known, due to the fact that District Attorney Gentry has not filed the informations but it is likely that they will be as follows:

The most prominent and one of the most interesting to the local people will be the trial of Mrs. Anne Bernard (Queen Ann) and Tom Yarberry for cattle rustling. Last year no decision was reached, although it is understood that the majority of the jury were for acquittal. Attorney Saunders, of Pueblo, who has the reputation of being the best lawyer ever heard in this part of the country will again have charge of the case for the defendants, assisted by A.M. Gooding.

During the many postponements of the new District Court Docket, Ann Bassett Bernard, naturally anxious to proceed with her court case, had recently completed another court case; her divorce from Hiram "Hi" Bernard. The divorce papers were filed by Hi Bernard, not Ann, citing desertion, on March 1, 1913.

Ann seemed to have no regrets over the failed marriage. Perhaps, given the age difference and the clash of personalities, she expected it would not last. Or, quite possibly she had achieved her goal in sabotaging Ora Haley's big cattle operation by stealing away his ranch manager. Ann wrote in her memoirs that she considered herself "set fast on the withers of the Two Bar." Hiram "Hi" Bernard likewise seemed to have few regrets. He later said: "Ann was a gay and exciting companion–too exciting I guess. A man does not enjoy playing second fiddle to so many things, like cattle and horses and dozens of other pets. A man wants to rate above a chipmunk and I could not make the grade."

As Ann's second trial began in August 1913, community sentiment swelled in Ann's favor. Remembering the connection of Ora Haley and the cattle barons' attempt to install Meldrum in the Routt County sheriff department, many citizens now began to realize that there could very well be a concerted effort in the worst way by Ora Haley and the Two Bar cattle company to frame Ann Bassett Bernard.

Thus, when Ann's trial began, the atmosphere among the spectators was more intense than the first trial. Again held in Craig, the courtroom was filled with Ann's many supporters who considered the trial as a showdown between the small ranch owners and the large cattle barons. Ann's supporters also included a large following of Craig women, as well as wives of area ranchers who traveled to Craig for the trial.

Following the selection of the jury, the evidence presented was nearly the same as the first trial. Ann's attorneys, A. M. Gooding and Miles G. Saunders, were only slightly hampered by their lack of witnesses for the defense. However, they still had their star witness: Ann herself. When the prosecuting attorney called Ora Haley to the stand, the trial took a decided turn. On cross examination, defense attorney Saunders asked Haley how many cattle he had in the county. With this direct question, Haley inadvertently admitted that he had lied to the county assessor. In answering the question, Haley paused a moment and then replied he had 10,000 head of cattle. Saunders then asked why his county assessor statement, filed four months previously, claimed assets of only 5,600 cattle and further asked if he had lied on that form. The prosecution objected, but Saunders had made his point and it did not go unnoticed by the jury. For the first time in Haley's career he had been humiliated in a public setting.

Again, J. S. Hoy offered his comments, often quite humorous as well as enlightening regarding the views of livestock during that era. Hoy wrote:

> The State called to the witness stand, W. M. Patton, foreman of the Two Bar at the time of the alleged beef-killing, also Detective Nelson. The latter testified to getting board and lodging at the Douglas Mountain Ranch,

owned by Mrs. Bernard, and while there doing a little gumshoe work, being rewarded by finding evidence of fresh butchering. He stated further that he returned to the Two Bar Ranch on Snake river, March 18 and reported his find to Foreman Patton, who with Ora McNurlen and John Patton, went to the scene and found the hide and offal of a freshly killed animal. The hide was hidden in the bushes and was afterward brought to Craig by Sheriff Ledford. From this hide the brand had been cut and shown in court along with the hocks that fitted the hide. Other witnesses stated that there were marks on the hide showing that it was the property of the Two Bar Ranch.

The following is the testimony of Ora Haley that was considered sensational. When Ora Haley was called to the stand, he became considerably "balled up" in regard to the manner in which the brand was placed upon the Haley cattle. He also stated that he was the sole owner, while the complaint stated that the animal killed belonged to the Haley Livestock and Trading Company. Another one of Haley's statements that caused considerable stir was that he had ten thousand cattle ranging in the Brown's Park country during 1911!!

It will be remembered that Haley is now threatening to sue the county for the recovery of tax assessment on a considerably less number of cattle!!! Mrs. Bernard in her testimony admitted about everything told about her except that she did not butcher one of Haley's heifers, and that at the time of the butchering, there were with her Tom Yarberry, Bill Malon, Mat Morelock and Ed Bassett, and that the heifer belonged to the last named individual.

Sensation Number Four. Three witnesses who appeared for Mrs. Bernard at the first trial, were conspicuous by their absence in this her second trial. They were "Chick" Bowen, Killed at Baggs, Wyoming, last year by Gunman Meldrum; Mat Morelock, who recently completed a term in the State Reformatory and has since left for parts unknown; and Pat Malone, who left the country secretly, about three steps ahead of the sheriff, last winter, being wanted for stealing sheep!!!!

187

During the taking of evidence Ora Haley was ordered outside the railing reserved for attorneys and their clients, Queen Ann's counsel objecting to his presence and close proximity to the jurors–being a desperate character when chasing criminals to their holes or running them out of the country.

The case of cattle rustling against Ann Bassett Bernard was given to the jury. After eight hours of deliberation, the jury returned a unanimous verdict of not guilty. The *Craig Courier* put out a special edition of their paper, the only time in its history to do so. The *Denver Post*, with a reporter in Craig, filed their story the following day:

BUSINESSES CLOSE, BANDS BLARE -
TOWN OF CRAIG GOES WILD WITH JOY

After deliberating over eight hours, the jury in the 'Queen Ann' cattle rustling case reported at 7:10 this evening. The verdict was not guilty. This is the third time this case has been tried and the trial has attracted the attention of the entire Northwestern Colorado. The courtroom was packed when the jury's decision became known and the crowd poured into the streets, shouting and throwing their hats into the air. Cowboy friends of Mrs. Bernard were out in force and the air rang with their revolver shots. Mrs. Bernard was placed in an automobile and paraded through the main streets of town receiving the congratulations and well wishes of her friends. This evening Mrs. Bernard rented the motion picture show and invited all to attend. She is also giving a free dance, and a monster banquet is being prepared at the leading hotel. The business houses of Craig are all closed and a brass band parades the streets in honor of Mrs. Bernard's release.

J. S. Hoy, with his disdain for small ranch owners and "homesteaders," later wrote:

The newspaper reporter concludes his account of the trial by saying: "Splendid talks were made by Judge Wiley in

188

behalf of the Livestock Association, and the talks made by Miles Saunders and Judge Chambers for the defense." Taking the trial altogether, it was a success, made so by an unusual display of legal talent, as bright and scintillating and varied as fireworks, combined with cuttlefish methods that muddied the legal waters, giving themselves an opportunity to escape all responsibility for a mis-carriage of justice, and make the innocent appear to be guilty, and the guilty innocent as charged in the indictment. A verdict of "Not guilty" was greeted with great applause by the spectators. The "criminal" attorneys in this case as in most other like cases where homesteaders or others without permanent homes were arrested for stealing cattle or horses, tried to make it appear that the defendant was being prosecuted and persecuted by cattlemen in an attempt to drive them off the public domain and out of the country.

After a decade, Ann's vendetta against Ora Haley ironically came to an end in a court of law instigated by Ora Haley himself. Ann's popularity only grew with her exoneration by a jury of her peers, while Ora Haley's popularity diminished and his one-time cattle empire suffered dramatically. Within a year of the trial Haley had sold his ranch on the Snake River and by the following year, he sold the rest of his Colorado holdings. A few years later, Bernard told Frank Willis just what he thought of Ora Haley:

He [Haley] is the direct cause of all of the tragedys that ever happened in Browns Park. We all practically came to the same drift fence in the end. Haley is paralyzed, and is being trundeled around in a wheel chair. I go around knocking my hocks because of a weak heart that kicks up a fuss and fails to pump regularly. I was only a machine for Haley. At any time, he oiled me up, and I ran smoothly for too many years. When I began to back fire and wanted a new steering gear Haley junked me. He accused me of double crossing him when I quit him to marry Ann Bassett. We had one hearty row and I haven't seen Haley since.

189

Throughout her lifetime, Ann never had a bad word to say about Hi Bernard. Despite the differences between the two, Bernard had helped in achieving another goal of Ann's, that of improving the Bassett ranch and extending the cattle herd. She later wrote:

> I became the wife of Hi Bernard (one of the West's most noted managers of two of the biggest outfits in Wyoming and Colorado,) a man who had carried on in that capacity for thirty years, in complete control of range activities. From my own experiences and observations, then from him, I learned that the grasping cattle barons of those early days were the biggest cattle thieves of all time.

Following the divorce, Bernard sold his homestead claim adjoining Ann's Douglas Mountain spread and moved on with his life. He lived with Eb Bassett for a time before leaving Brown's Park. Ann wrote:

> Elbert Bassett maintained a free home at the old Bassett Ranch, a spot where the birds and the beasts, homeless, travel-wearied mankind, all found a refuge, food and shelter, given in kindness and without reservation. I am glad that my brother "Eb" took Hi Bernard there, when the sands of his life were running low.

Hi Bernard drifted between various ranch jobs as he could find them. Eventually he would return to Northwestern Colorado, buying a small bunch of cattle in partnership with the former Routt County sheriff, Joe Jones, the same man Ann had once held a gun on.

As for "Queen" Ann Bassett, she was ready to get on with her life and a bit of quiet solitude.

CHAPTER NOTES AND SOURCE INFORMATION

Ann Bassett Willis' life experiences appeared in a four-part series published in the Colorado Historical Society's *Colorado Magazine*. The series, titled, "Queen Ann of Brown's Park," ran in Volume XXIX January 1952, Volume XXIX April 1952, Volume XXIX October 1952, Volume XXX January 1953. They are available at the Denver Public Library, as well as the Museum of Northwest Colorado, Craig, Colorado. Unless otherwise noted, the quotes attributed to Ann are from this work.

Justice of the Peace, Z. Z. Carpenter's subpoena for Anna M. Bassett to appear before him, dated March 29, 1911, including his handwritten instructions, is found in the archives of the Museum of Northwest Colorado, Craig, Colorado.

The case of the State of Colorado vs. Anna Bernard and Thomas Yarberry, filed August 8, 1911, is found in the Moffat County Court records.

Contrary to many writers who have attributed the "Queen Ann" reference to a *Denver Post* reporter, it was first used in the *Craig Empire* issue of April 1, 1911.

Esther Campbell's quote regarding Ann's moniker, "Queen," can be found in her letters archived at the Bureau of Land Management, Vernal, Utah. Also see DeJournette, Dick and Daun, *One Hundred Years of Brown's Park and Diamond Mountain*, pg. 237.

Josie's account of her sister's 'Queen Ann' moniker is from her taped interviews, held at the Dinosaur National Monument, Jensen, Utah. Typewritten account is available at the Museum of Northwest Colorado, Craig, Colorado.

J. S. Hoy's comments are from his unpublished manuscript, *History of Brown's Park*, 1917.

Bob Meldrum was convicted of the murder of Chick Bowen and sentenced to prison at the Wyoming State Penitentiary. He was later pardoned.

The case of the State of Colorado vs. Anna Bernard and Thomas Yarberry, was filed August 9 1913, two years later, and almost to the day. The records are found in the Moffat

County Court House, and copies are available at the Museum of Northwest Colorado, Craig, Colorado.

Hiram H. Bernard's petition for divorce, citing, "Desertion, without fault of said plaintiff, (Ann Bernard) for more than one year last past," is found at the Moffat County Courthouse archives. A copy is also available at the Museum of Northwest Colorado.

Despite the reporting of the *Denver Post*, Ann Bassett Bernard was only tried twice in the case of cattle rustling.

Hiram "Hi" Bernard's quotes are from *Confidentially Told*, the unpublished manuscript by Frank Willis. Willis spent the summer of 1917 with Bernard, caring for cattle near the Green River, west of the Bassett ranch.

THE FINAL YEARS

Following Ann's sensational trial and subsequent acquittal, she returned to her ranch on Douglas Mountain where rumors of cattle rustling again floated over the Park. While Ann allowed her ranch to be used as a stopover for rustlers bringing cattle over the border from Utah, she never participated in rustling cattle.

Ann took a much needed vacation. She and her elderly father made the trip to her sister Josie's ranch on Cub Creek in Utah. Ann liked the area and bought a land claim on South Fork, some five miles from Josie's ranch. Herb helped build a small cabin for his daughter on the property. For a while, Ann divided her time between her Utah homestead and her ranch in Brown's Park.

During one trip back to Brown's Park, Ann rekindled a longtime relationship with Francis "Frank" Willis. The two had known each other for years through Frank's friendship with Hi Bernard. In fact, some four years after Hi and Ann were divorced, Willis and Bernard were working together, looking after cattle along the Green River, near Lodore Canyon. One day during that hot summer of 1917, Bernard found himself in a situation which led to fisticuffs, defending Ann's honor. The brawl was with none other than J. S. Hoy, another old-time nemesis of Ann's. Willis recounted the incident in *Confidentially Told*, his unpublished memoir largely based on reminisces of his old friend, and Ann's ex-husband, Hiram "Hi" Bernard. Willis wrote:

> One day in midsummer, right out of nowhere came a visitor, the elderly, highly educated James Shade Hoy. An excentric recluse who lived three miles to the north and on the opposite side of the river. Hoy was one of the

Following her acquittal of cattle rustling, Ann Bassett continued to ride the range. *Museum of Northwest Colorado*

early settlers of Browns Park. Upon his arrival, according to rules of western hospitality, preparations for dinner was started, and to have a little extra special service for a guest, I went to the garden and picked a small pail of luscious ripe strawberries. Mr. Hoy offered to wash and hull the berries.

When we were seated at the dinner table, the conversation drifted around to Browns Park history, and to Hoys recital of how he had written articles to various newspapers, and to the governors of Colorado, Utah and Wyoming, suggesting ways and means to rid the country of migratory criminals. My protests were in vain he said until my brother Valentine Hoy was shot and killed by Harry Tracy..."And that," remarked Hoy, "was the the beginning of the end of outlawry in Browns Park." At that point Bernard took up the conversation and added, "Yes Hoy, you overstressed the desirability of Browns Park as a perfect and secure retreat for thieves and outlaws. Hoy–your writings, many of them widely circulated, advertised the place that otherwise would never have been known to exist. Some of your writings gave all of the in habitants of the Park, yourself included, the reputation of being thieves and crooks of every description. A man that would write and publish such stuff about his own community, a place where he has lived for over forty years, and has valuable interests, is a dam fool...Your publications are the foundations for a grave injustice to the people of this section. I will refer you to one article in particular. Quoting you, 'Browns Park is a den of unclean beasts and a roost for unclean birds.' In this writing you make no exceptions, you classify your neighbors, your brothers and their families, all in one melting Pot of criminality. You have been sending such messages for twenty years or longer."

Hoy gave a shocked reply. "Bernard, you are not a gentleman. And who are you to make such accusations? We the People of Browns Park have endured the slings of suffering hardships...but we never disgraced, humiliated and insulted until you dragged your swimish carcass across our fair land."

The argument was gaining momentum by leaps. Bernard quickly picked up and opened fire. "Hoy you are the first cattle thief to enter your fair land. You stole a bunch of cattle belonging to the Interior Department and headed them to Browns Park. In 1870, your outfit was picked up in Wyoming by Secret Service Agents and the stolen stock recovered. To keep out of Federal Prison you sailed to Europe and remained for several years. When your brother, Valentine Hoy, was killed you were too cowardly to go with the posses to bring in the body, you hid in your house until Mrs. Warren and Josie McKnight coaxed you out."

Again Hoy struck back, and hit the bulls eye. "Bernard, you beetle-browed scoundrel, you hired Tom Horn to kill our respectable citizens to gain a footing in this country, when that failed, you married Ann Bassett one of our outstanding girls to further your greedy cause." To emphasize that heavy blow below the belt, Hoy emotionally beat the table with his fist and sent the food-laden dishes spinning to the floor, with a loud crash, as he shouted, "how could she so disgrace Browns Park? How could she?"

That question was to be answered by both men, as they stumbled for their guns. I stepped quickly into an adjoining room and cached the deadly weapons in a closet and returned to the scene of action. The old codgers were throwing rights and lefts at each other with might and fury.

The fight then developed into a scratching, hair pulling contest. Bernard who was partially bald, stole the show in hair handicap, as Hoy had an abundance of hair. When Bernard got a good hold of and began to pull I expected to see a toupe lifted from Hoys pate, but I was disappointed, the hair stuck. I had been told that he wore a wig, but this pulling incident was convincing evidence that I had been misinformed—for at each jerk Hoy would let out a blasphemous yell of indignation.

Following the trial, Ann and her father vacationed at Josie's place at Cub Creek, Utah. From left is Josie's son Crawford, Ann, two neighbors and Herb Bassett. This is believed to be the last known photograph of Herb Bassett.

Uintah County Libary, Vernal, Utah

As the summer of 1917 came to a close Bernard and Willis began making plans to separate their cattle herds and move them to a warmer climate for the winter. According to Willis, one day in a casual conversation, Bernard made the following statement to him:

> Ebb Bassett said that Ann is coming home to visit in the fall. I know the answers to that. Ann is not so much interested in seeing any human being as she is in rambling over the old Bassett Ranch and caressing every ugly, scraggy cedar in Browns Park. She is blended into the rugged mountains around here and belongs to them.
>
> Of course I'll be the happiest old fool in the world when I see her, and cuss myself for it.

It is not known whether Ann and Hi ever met when Ann returned to Brown's Park that fall; Ann does not say. It is also not known if Willis ever related the conversation to Ann, or the brawl

Ann's hand-written request for proof of water right ownership.
Museum of Northwest Colorado

between Bernard and J. S. Hoy, which Bernard started in defense of Ann's honor. From Bernard's conversation with Willis, it is clear that he still had deep feelings for Ann. Yet, what would ultimately transpire between Willis and Anne following their reconnection later that same year, leads one to believe that Willis probably stayed mum on both incidents.

Francis "Frank" Willis, an engineering surveyor, first came to the area in 1900 where he was employed by Rocky Mountain Fuel Company. His surveying skills were a great asset in the construction of the new mountain road over Rabbit Ears

Pass, south of Steamboat Springs in Routt County. Following the completion of the road, Willis remained in the area, finding work punching cows for the Two Circle Bar. In 1904, he went to work for Ora Haley's Two Bar cattle operation, under the management of Bill Patton. This was during the time that Patton was learning of the warring factions between Ann Bassett and Ora Haley. Patton offered Willis 500 dollars to quit the Two Circle Bar job and go to work at the Bassett ranch in an effort to gather evidence of cattle rustling. Willis not only refused the offer but quit the Two Circle Bar. After working in Nebraska and Wyoming, Willis returned to Brown's Park in 1917 where he and Ann resumed their friendship, which led to a courtship.

It was during this time that a sad event diverted Ann's attention. On July 30, 1918, Ann's father, Amos Herbert Bassett died at a veteran soldiers home in Quincy, Illinois. The August 29, 1918, issue of the *Moffat County Mirror* carried his obituary:

> Word was received recently of the death of A. H. Bassett, at the Soldiers Home near, Quincy, Illinois. He had been with his daughters, Mrs. Morris and Mrs. Bernard, the past year. In June he went to the soldiers home in Illinois mainly to be under medical treatment for a while.
>
> On July 20th he had a severe stroke of paralysis and lived only a few hours. Word failed to reach the family in time, so he was given a military burial at the home.
>
> It was not possible for any of his children to be with him when the end came. He leaves five children, Mrs. Josie Morris, Jensen, Utah, Sam Bassett, Alaska, Mrs. Anna M. Bernard, Elbert and George Bassett, Lodore, Colorado.

Ann was understandably devastated by the loss of her beloved father and her grief was quite upsetting. Eventually, with the help of Frank Willis, Ann worked through this trying time.

Willis had an easy-going personality, something very much needed to handle Ann's flighty nature. He liked to sing and play the banjo and Ann loved his stories of roaming the range herding cattle. It proved to be a perfect match when 37 year-old Frank

The Bassett family ranch. *Museum of Northwest Colorado*

Willis married the 42 year-old Ann Bassett Bernard in 1923. Not long after the wedding, Willis got the itch to roam the country again and Ann was more than willing to do a bit of traveling. Reflecting years later on leaving Brown's Park, Ann wrote:

> I would avoid being smothered by fences, and the digging up, where every sagebrush, gulch and rock had a meaning of its own, and each blade of grass or scrubby cedar was a symphony. I could make effective my escape. If I had to be hedged in by people I would go away to the crowded cities, to mingle with the human herd and study them from the sidelines, for I had no desire to become a part of their affairs. All I asked of life was to be perpetually let alone, to go my way undisturbed. To Brown's Park and its hills and valleys (the only thing I had ever selfishly loved) I bade goodbye.

As the Willis couple was making their plans to travel west, Ann learned of the death of her ex-husband, Hiram "Hi" Bernard. Ann had always held Bernard in high esteem. The *Craig Empire* reported the death in the February 26, 1924, issue:

> Hi Bernard, Browns park ranchman and stock raiser, walked into a restaurant at Rock Springs, Wyo., Thursday after having ridden for several hours, and suddenly collapsed, death being instantaneous. Every old timer in this section knew Hi Bernard. He left his native Texas home at the age of 14, punching cattle on the northward trail. About 50 years ago he was with a cattle outfit at Sweetwater, 15 or 20 years later coming to this section, where he was foreman for the Two-Bar. Hi Bernard was known as the wisest cattleman in Northwestern Colorado, a man absolutely fearless and a leader among men. About 15 years ago he married Miss Anne Bassett, but they separated after a few years. Bernard was about 70 years old. Burial was at Rock Springs Sunday.

The Willis' went to California where Frank worked in the oil fields for the Richfield Oil company and Ann ran the Cooper Hotel in Huntington Beach. In 1928, Josie's son Chick McKnight and his wife Edith moved to Huntington Beach. McKnight had lived in California for some time and even worked as a stunt rider in Hollywood movies.

It was here in California that Ann received the news, in 1925, that her younger brother, Elbert "Eb" Bassett had committed suicide in Brown's Park. Ann was quite saddened by the news and stunned to learn that the cause may have been losing the family ranch over financial debt. She was never informed and had no idea that her brother was in trouble or that the Bassett family ranch was at risk. The *Craig Courier* ran the following headline in the November 19, 1925, issue of the paper:

201

Lodore Rancher Suicides

Eben Bassett of Brown's Park Took Poison at home of Frank Lawrence on Big Gulch early Thursday Morning.

Was one of Pioneer Cattlemen of Northwestern Colorado as to have appeared in Court today to answer charge of killing cow.

Elbert "Eb" Bassett had been involved in a few underhanded dealings and was heavily in debt. In an effort to save the Bassett family ranch, Eb had deeded it to his brother George. When Eb was investigated for fraud, the judge ruled that deeding the ranch to George was an effort to hide assets and Eb lost the family ranch. Josie believed Eb was remorseful for losing the ranch and "just grew tired of living." Crawford, Josie's son, however, later said that he was in love with a woman "he could never have." However, the *Craig Courier* reported added details in the November 25, 1925 issue, with the headline:

Ann and Frank Willis lived in this cabin following their marriage in 1923.
Uintah County Libary, Vernal, Utah

Dies With His Boots Off

No one but me knows or suspects what I am going to do, no one.
(Signed Eb Bassett.)

This was the note that led to finding the body of Eb Bassett at the Frank Lawrence ranch on lower Big Gulch last Thursday morning. Bassett, W. E. Sweet and Ed Ainge were on their way to Craig to appear before the Justice of the Peace. It was noted that Bassett was missing when the others rose in the morning but nothing was thought of the matter until the note was found and this led to the discovery of the body. Bassett evidently had the old time superstition in regard to dying with his boots on and had removed them before taking the fatal dose. The body was brought to Craig at once and an inquest and autopsy was held with the verdict "died from taking poisons into the stomach."

Because Ann was in California, it was left to the eldest Bassett sibling, Josie, to travel to Brown's Park. There, she made the arrangements for her brother's funeral. A small service for Elbert "Eb" Bassett was held, followed by burial in the Bassett family cemetery.

In his will, Eb left the few assets he had, particularly cattle, to his older sisters, Josie and Ann. Josie rounded up what was left of Eb's cattle. She arrived in Zenobia Basin in Brown's Park on a chilly November day. As she gathered the cattle for the long trip back to her ranch on Cub Creek, a few local ranchers watched and checked that none of the animals had their brands. It was then that she realized Eb's reputation in the Park was not a good one.

Years later, George Bassett's daughter, Edna Bassett Haworth, remarked about the bond between the two brothers:

As far back as my knowledge goes, Eb did many things, terrible things, that were extremely hurtful and expensive, Dad seemed to take it all stoically, trying to smooth things

203

over, make amends. They were friends, they worked together some, saw a good deal of each other, and I know Dad was fond of Eb, making it that much harder for him to bear Eb's transgressions.

During their time in California, Ann and Frank received a visit from an old friend of Ann's. Edith McKnight Jensen, the wife of Ann's nephew, Chick McKnight, later recalled the occasion:

Queen Ann was running a little rooming house for the oil workers at Huntington Beach, California. Chick and I were running a riding academy over near Hermosa Beach. Ann called and asked us to come down the next weekend. She mentioned Elza Lay was coming to visit and bringing his wife and children along, too.

Chick and I went to Ann's place. Elza, his wife

Herbert "Eb" Bassett was buried in the family cemetery above the Bassett ranch. *Museum of Northwest Colorado*

[Mary,] and two children, [James and Mary Lucille] were already there. They were well dressed and very pleasant to visit with. I have to admit, I was never around nicer people. Elza didn't look like a bank robber. His appearance was more that of a banker.

Every few years the Willis' managed to visit family and friends in Brown's Park. The summer of 1929 was their first trip back since the death of Ann's brother, Eb. The *Craig Empire* reported the visit in the June 19, 1929, issue:

Mr. and Mrs. Frank Willis of Huntington Beach, Calif., were Craig visitors last week. Mrs. Willis will be remembered by Moffat county pioneers as "Queen Anne" Bernard, who was at one time the principal figure of the most sensational court trial ever held in Craig. At that time she was acquitted of butchering 2-Bar beef. Mr. and Mrs. Willis now conduct a big apartment house in the California city.

Undoubtedly, Ann spent time at the family cemetery, where Eb had been buried near his mother Elizabeth. After nearly seven years in California, the Willis' were ready to move on. The local Huntington Beach newspaper ran the following article:

Local Woman Will Manage Sheep Ranch in Nevada

Here is a surprise for Huntington Beach. For some time this city has been the home of a quiet matronly woman whom no one suspected was a capable sheep raiser. For years she tried to be domestic—and now she has returned to her native calling. Mrs. Frank Willis, who for several years has so efficiently managed the Cooper hotel, has recently formed a company of three women for the purpose of going into the sheep business. The corporation has leased 480 acres at St. Thomas, Nevada, with a wider range of government land adjacent. Mrs. Willis is leaving on

Saturday to become active manager of the business. She has purchased five hundred sheep, but contemplates adding a hundred more to the ranch soon. Mr. Willis, who is with the Richfield Oil company, will remain here for a time.

Following their brief stint at sheep ranching, the couple moved to Arizona, where they lived in the Walapai Valley near Kingman, Arizona. Ann took classes in forestry management at the University of Arizona, until she learned that the U. S. Forest Service did not accept women as forest rangers. Ann later wrote: "For the slapdash reason I happened to be a female, I was forced to withdraw my application. I am still protesting that law." In 1931, the couple purchased a cattle ranch and built a home at Hackberry,

Elza Lay and his family paid a visit to his old friend Ann Bassett while she and Frank were living in California. *Museum of Northwest Colorado*

Arizona. Chick and Edith McKnight joined them and the two couples worked as partners in the ranch operations. Over time it was a fairly successful ranch with 1,200 head of cattle. About 18 months later, McKnight was involved in a terrible automobile accident. With his neck broken in three places, he was out of commission for the next two years. As this was the height of the Great Depression, and the Willis ranch struggling financially, McKnight's absence forced Frank and Ann Willis to sell out in 1937.

The couple returned

to Colorado, where Frank obtained employment with the Bureau of Mines. This job required travel, and Frank and Ann moved around the states of Colorado and Wyoming. As time permitted between jobs, the Willis' traveled to Josie's place on Cub Creek and occasionally visited at Brown's Park.

In February 1943, the couple was in Afton, Wyoming. At the height of World War II, when America desperately needed metal and mineral resources, Frank was busy with his job with the Bureau of Mines. Meanwhile, Ann had just completed a rough draft of her memoir, *Scars and Two Bars*. She had sent excerpts to the *Moffat County Mirror*, which would publish

The eldest of the Bassett children, Josephine, "Josie," made the arrangements for her brother Eb's funeral and drove his cattle from Colorado to her ranch at Cub Creek, Utah.
Museum of Northwest Colorado

them beginning in April. Meanwhile, Ann wrote a letter to the *Moffat County Mirror*, touting the efforts of the Bureau for which her husband worked. The newspaper published the letter in the February 25, 1943, issue:

> The following letter was received from Mrs. Ann Bassett Willis former resident of the Brown's Park area. Mrs. Willis is now at Afton, Wyoming, where her husband is employed with the Bureau of Mines, whose job is to keep the United States supplied with the vital metals such as vanadium. As she remarks, the Bureau of Mines is "in there

pitching" toward the final victory.

This arm of our much discussed Bureaus, the Bureau of Mines, is under manned, and in "pitching" capable, resolute, exploration engineer, Forest Majors and his unbeatable assistants are burrowing into the black phosphate, earnestly searching out the precious vanadium, a mineral vital to the war program. Afton, Wyo., a rural community of fourteen hundred inhabitants that has given five hundred men and boys to the Armed Forces, and over two hundred girls to essential industries, need not be reminded of total war. Ann Bassett Willis.

While Ann worked side by side with her husband supporting the war effort, she remained heartsick over both the death of her brother Eb and the loss of the family ranch. However, in discussions with her brother George, who retained some of the outlying acreage, she learned that other original Bassett acres were now considered public domain. Ann sprang into action, filing a

Following Eb's suicide, his brother George took over the family ranch. *Museum of Northwest Colorado*

Ann and Frank Willis. *Museum of Northwest Colorado*

request to buy the land for its historic value. In 1944, she eventually received title to nearly 39 acres of land. The land included the old log cabin, where Eb's girlfriend Mattie Edwards still lived, as well as the flowing spring and the orchard Ann's parents had planted. Ann later wrote: "Many years went by before I returned to my 'sacred cow,' Brown's Park. I was surprised to find so many pretty little homes tucked away in the hills."

However, returning to the place where she was born, grew up, and fought for years to defend, brought back the memories of her vendetta against Ora Haley and the Two Bar ranch. Ann later wrote: "Brown's Park brought back a poignant yearning to dash away and drive an avalanche of Two Bar cattle back across the divide. Then I would awaken from my dream to discover that I had been peeping into the past that cannot return. Live Two Bar cattle are conspicuously absent. The winds have buried all the dead ones."

Frank and Ann Willis built a cabin of their own next to the old cabin where Mattie was living. Ann was polite and sympathetic with Mattie at first. After a few months the woman began to irritate Ann, and she asked Mattie to move out of the cabin. A few weeks

After Ann regained title to a portion of the family ranch, she and Frank built a cabin of their own on the Bassett ranch. *Uintah County Libary, Vernal, Utah*

went by and Ann asked again. After a few months of Mattie's extended loitering, Ann had had enough. One day when Mattie had made a trip to Craig, Ann burned down the cabin. She was nice enough, however, to place Mattie's meager possessions outside of the cabin before she lit the match.

Ann's happiest times had always been at her beloved Brown's Park and now she could enjoy her time there, carefree with her husband Frank. As she grew older, the winters were harder to bear. She and Frank spent the winter months in the small southwestern town of Leeds, Utah. Although the couple was in their retirement years, they enjoyed prospecting for low-grade silver ore at the old abandoned Silver Reef mine near Leeds. Over the years they not only found great enjoyment in their hobby, but made enough money to supplement their income.

Happy, relaxed, and enjoying her golden years, Ann resumed another passion: writing. In her youth she had always kept a diary and enjoyed writing long letters to family and friends. She became incensed at the many inaccuracies written regarding the history of Brown's Park. The citizens were often portrayed as rustlers and thieves. Her own family reputation was sullied in many publications. In Ann's opinion, the worst of these books were Charles Kelly's 1938 book, *Outlaw Trail: The Story of Butch Cassidy,* and W. G. Tittsworth's 1927 book, *Outskirt Episodes*, in which fabricated actions were attributed to Isom Dart without basis. The characters in the book were given fictitious names such as the evil "Nat Rasper" who was actually Matt Rash. Ann was particularly outraged at this mischaracterization of her deceased fiancé.

Willis-% U.S.Bureau of Mines.
Thermopolis, Wyo.

Salt Lake City, Utah
April 21st 1944

Dear Edna;
 I am saying damn, damn,this morning because I am not getting to see you folks on this trip. We have to go by way of Rawlins to reach Thermopolis for the simple reason that South Pass is not open and it is not one mile farther to go by Craig ,we have been ordered to go by Evanston, then by Rock Springs to Rawlins; You will understand the gas plays a very important role in our movements just now, otherwise I would tell the G.I's to go to hell and do as I please but in this issue the old gal is handicaped. No gas, only hot air and plenty of that but it wont move a car. So-----saysI.

 I wrote to Geo telling him to take Mattie or leave her as he saw fit. I rather think he will see fit if he doesn't have one. How in heavens name can one lease any Govt. land that they did not have the slightest title or right to lease it.
 Dear little Mattie saw how nice it was to burn the build ings and leave her self out in the cold. I cant see it any other way.
 I have a very nice letter from Lu, he is fine and said he got your Christmas letter. He seemed to be pleased to hear from you. Dr John is married and has a boy baby. He is stationed in the U.S. Can you beat it and Lu has to stay in dirty old Italy until every thing is over, if it is ever so.

Ann's letter, dated 1944, to George's daughter regarding the Bassett property.
Museum of Northwest Colorado

Ann was also resentful of Kelly's portrayal of Tom Horn and the murders of her fiancé Matt Rash and Isom Dart, committed in Brown's Park. Ann wrote:

Thirty-five years after the Tom Horn murder trial, Charles Kelly wrote a book, Outlaw Trail. Mr. Kelly did not attend that trial, but he places his personal stamp of approval upon Horn's activities and pits his judgment against that of selected and sworn jurymen. The jurymen Kelly superficially passes off as "nesters" were twelve men

211

of the city of Cheyenne, charged with the duty of sitting through a lengthy court proceedings and hearing all of the evidence presented for both sides of the case. They heard the examination of testimony as given by the witnesses and the judge's final instructions to the jury. After all these years, Kelly questions the integrity of the men who had the stamina to weigh all the evidence in the balance and mete out just punishment to the self-acknowledged murderer, Tom Horn.

In Kelly's book, among the many distortions was this outrageous claim regarding Ann's many deeds:

Children grew into young men and woman without benefit of education, except what little they may have had forced upon them in Charley Crouse's school house. Young men naturally became expert rustlers, but they were not to be outdone by the girls. "Queen Anne," according to stories told in the Hole, once stole a herd of five hundred cattle single-handed and drove them to the railroad where they were sold. Her exploit was conducted from the front seat of a covered wagon, the team being used as saddle horses as required.

Of course this was an absurd account on many levels. First, the school house "in the Hole,' as Kelly wrote, was not Crouse's, but started by Ann's father, Herb, in 1881, the same year Ann's mother, Elizabeth, successfully had the name changed from Brown's Hole to Brown's Park. Second, not Ann, nor any other person, male or female, could or would be able to steal "single-handed" such a large herd of cattle. Nor would the individual be able to keep such a herd in order from the "seat of a covered wagon."

Ann deeply resented this false claim regarding her character and integrity. Therefore, Ann set out to write her own account of her life and the history of Brown's Park. Many of her writings survive in published forums such as the Colorado Historical Society's *Colorado History Magazine*, as well as portions of her unpublished memoirs, titled *Scars and Two Bars.* Excerpts of this manuscript were published in the *Moffat Mirror* newspaper in 1943.

Ann began corresponding with an old acquaintance from Utah, Esther Campbell. Soon, Esther spent the summers with Ann in Brown's Park, where they worked on a story of Ann's life

Esther Anderson Campbell, a life long friend of Ann's and later Josie's as well, wrote many articles regarding the lives of her friends.
Uintah County Libary, Vernal, Utah

for a possible Hollywood film, of which Samuel Goldwyn had expressed an interest. As the friendship developed, Esther also met Ann's sister, Josie. Esther wanted to bring Josie in on the writing collaboration. In a letter to Esther, Ann responded regarding her sister's involvement:

> I have thought for a long time that someone would make a picture of Brown's Park historical background. The one thing I have been afraid of was it might be taken from "Outlaw Trail" and that fact has worried me. The damned stuff Kelley put out was senseless and stupid and still people sucked it up. No doubt we could furnish more real more exciting and far more interesting historical facts if given a

chance...Josie puts all the little episodes of our daily lives in those early times down as too trivial and nonsensical for people to be interested in. She just shrugs it off and says "Of course Jack Rolla was killed so was Valentine Hoy. What of it—we buried them and that's the end of it. Why start that all over again." While I think all those things are important in a country's history, Josie says nuts to me. She knows its all true but thinks its' silly to write or tell it now after so many years. Speaking plainly, Josie won't be worth a tinkers damn to us on history. She will fit in as an old resident of the "Hole" and that is all.

Ann further explained the vision she had in mind for work she and Esther were doing:

> I write not for publication but for the generations of [the] Bassett clan who had read absurd publications lacking in even a shade of truth. I had Sam's boys and their children as well as more distant relations in mind.
>
> I have lived in the Brown's Park and Douglas Mtn. country when and if you got a nice little outfit together just as you have by hard work and honestly, you would become a "cow thief." Rumor would be started floating around Denver, then spring up in Baggs and around Rawlins—seep to Vernal, etc. Then let the axe fall. The papers would slyly hint good riddance. Whisper "The Campbells were cow thieves did you know that?" "Well I heard it." "I did not believe it at first but—I guess it must be true, they got killed for it—I guess."
>
> Yes, I guess—it took guts and gumption to hold out and there was no guess work about that. Some of us were so mad and we failed to see the danger. Injustice loomed above every thought of safety.
>
> Hells bells I get strung out & can't quit, when Tom is mentioned. I go off my trolley and see red. Shut her down Ann you bore me. So Long.

Bill Tittsworth could have written a true story of the country and made it good history if he had been inclined that way. Mr. [Leroy] Hafen [Director of the Colorado Historical Society, and editor of The *Colorado Magazine*] had read all that stuff. He also has J. S. Hoy's manuscript. He told me that he could not publish it until he had worked it over and cut out the wicked personal venom that is so very obvious in Hoy's writing.

I don't expect you to take up the subject of the casteration of J. S. Hoy in your history. However, your club gals would be interested altho seeming to be very much shocked.

I could tell you a lot of such stuff. It would not be pretty. Some juicy scandal but I am not going to. I could implicate my self in some of the dirt. Some is funny. I am not going to do that either.

Perhaps Ann still held a grudge against Josie from a previous incident involving national publicity. In 1948, *Life* magazine ran an article on Josie. Ann and her husband Frank were visiting Josie at Cub Creek during this time and drove Josie to Vernal for the interview. In dressing for the interview, there was a stark contrast between the sisters as Ann was dressed in high fashion and Josie wore overalls, a felt hat, and tennis shoes. Ann was appalled at her sister's appearance. However, Josie had been told, and Ann had not, that the photo shoots would include Josie on horseback, photos of her with a shotgun, and photos of her shooting.

During the interview, the *Life* magazine editor even mentioned that the story could possibly become a Hollywood movie. Ann must have been jealous that her sister was about to get national attention for her life as a rancher, although, at the time, she never let on. The sibling rivalry that had always existed between the sisters simmered anew within Ann. When the article was published with the title of "Queen of the Rustlers," Ann was enraged.

Despite the time and work Ann and Esther put into their endeavor for the Hollywood mogul, Samuel Goldwyn, the "picture" never came to fruition. However, Josie would later get the last laugh with the sister rivalry, years after Ann's death. In 1967, Hollywood did make a film loosely based on a Bassett–Josie. It was titled "The Ballad of Josie," with Doris Day in the starring role. It was nothing close to Josie's life, but made for good box office receipts.

During the summer of 1949, Ann and Frank spent many warm days roaming around the Park and reminiscing. On one such outing at her family ranch, Ann had Frank dug up the old fence pole that had been used to hang John Jack "Judge" Bennett in 1898. Later, during a visit with her dear friend Esther Campbell and her husband Duward, Ann presented the fence pole to the Campbells as a gift. Ann told Esther she wanted her to have it: "Because anyone there [Brown's Park] not knowing what it was would just use it for branding fire, probably."

In the spring of 1953, Frank and Ann were at their cabin in Brown's Park when Ann suffered a severe heart attack. She was airlifted by helicopter to the Craig Memorial Hospital. Frank, worried

An older Ann Bassett Bernard Willis. *Museum of Northwest Colorado*

Ann and Frank Willis often visited Ann's older sister Josie at her cabin at Cub Creek, Utah. *Museum of Northwest Colorado*

sick over his beloved wife, never left the hospital. He notified Ann's favorite grandniece, Betty, who notified her father, Crawford McKnight. McKnight brought his mother Josie to Craig from her cabin on Cub Creek. When Josie entered the hospital room where Ann lay near death, she wept. Betty and Frank were at the bedside. Betty later said of the event that she had never seen her strong, tough grandmother cry. Josie sat by Ann's bed and held her hand for hours.

Ann, true to her obstinate nature, was anything but a patient patient. She yelled expletives at the nurses and threw things across the room. Finally she compelled Frank and Betty to obtain a vehicle that could transport her to her home in Leeds, Utah. Ann told Betty, "I shall not spend one more night in this filthy hole."

By September 1953, Ann, who had been recuperating at her home in Leeds, felt well enough to write a letter to Esther:

> The truth is I am very much out of the running right now. About two months ago I was hit by a rather serious heart condition which has set down a lot. If I do the slightest bit of arm exercise I go into a tail spin for sure. Then it's

Ann Bassett Willis. *Museum of Northwest Colorado*

Ann and Frank enjoy looking through old pictures in their cabin in Leeds, Utah. This is believed to be the last photograph of Ann Bassett Bernard Willis. *Museum of Northwest Colorado*

reach for the nitro-glycerine pill and slip it quickly under the tongue to get action. Dr. ordered me to quit work for awhile—or else—ten minutes or less can wind up the tick in an old body. It does not bother me any, its very painful so I do the heavy sitting slotting around and Frank does the work, not much to do.

Rosalie Miles DeJournette had continued her dear friendship with Ann Bassett since they first met when Rosalie was nine years-old. The two women traveled for visits as often as possible. Rosalie later wrote:

> In later years, Ann and Frank Willis came to Vernal and visited with me several times. They were living in Leeds, Utah. The last visit I had with Queen Ann was at my home in Vernal. We reminisced about the good times we spent together in Brown's Park and also Vernal. I might have been a snip of a girl, but I enjoyed every minute I spent with her.
>
> On our last visit I remember telling Ann I felt my parents thought Brown's Park was the "Promised Land" to them, with the mild winters, abundance of wild game and grassy meadows along the Green River.
>
> As Ann and I chatted that day, I noticed her health was starting to fail her. This last visit wasn't long before she died in 1956. With a bit of dampness around my eyes, I glanced at her thinking, "Thank You Queen Ann, thank you for being so kind to me. You helped make Brown's Park my Garden of Eden."

Ann, as stubborn and headstrong as she was, knew her health was declining. She wrote out her will leaving her Brown's Park land to her husband, Frank Willis, and her brother Sam's son, Emerson Bassett, with the stipulation that the land be passed down to future Bassetts and never to be sold. She also requested that she be cremated, and that her remains be spread across her beloved birthplace of Brown's Park.

219

On May 8, 1956, Ann Bassett Bernard Willis died at her home in Leeds, Utah, just days before her 79th birthday. Ann's dear friend, Esther Campbell, provided the Craig *Empire Courier* with Ann's obituary which was printed in the May 16, 1956, issue:

Ann Bassett Willis Dies At 79 After Interesting Life

The following information on Mrs. Willis's life was compiled and submitted to the Empire-Courier by Mrs. D. E. Campbell.

Mrs. Ann Bassett Willis, who was a former Moffat County resident and who helped make Brown's Park History, died at her home in Leeds, Utah, [last] Wednesday evening, three days before her 79th birthday.

Mrs. Willis had suffered from a heart ailment for several years. After a severe heart attack in September, 1953, she became a patient at the Craig Memorial Hospital for about three weeks after having spent the summer at her old home in Brown's Park. She never fully regained her strength.

Esther Campbell's account of Ann's heart attack is a bit faulty. Perhaps the obituary was prepared in haste and Esther, obviously grieving over the death of a dear friend, was a bit frazzled. In any case, Ann's 1953 heart attack occurred in the spring of that year. Ann wrote a letter to Esther dated September 1953, during her recuperation at her home in Leeds.

The obituary went on to recount Ann's birth in Brown's Park in 1878, the first white child born in the region, and included her marriages to Hiram "Hi" Bernard and Francis "Frank" Willis. Following a list of survivors, including her husband Frank, sister Josie, and several nephews and one niece, the article ended with the burial information: "Mrs. Willis requested cremation. Her ashes will be placed in the Bassett cemetery on the old home Bassett ranch in Brown's Park and be allowed to blow to the four winds. Her round-up days are over. Her heart has ever been in Brown's Park. She will be returned to its hills and valleys of which she herself has said "the only thing I ever selfishly loved.""

LAST WILL AND TESTAMENT

I, Ann Bassett Willis, being of sound mind and disposing memory, do declare this to be my Last Will and Testament.

I am the sole owner of the land and improvements on same, herein described: Lots in Sec. 34. T. 10, R. 102 W, 6 P.M. in Moffat County, Colorado. Said land is free of all encumbrances and it shall remain so.

At my death the property shall be under the control of Frank M. Willis who has full right to live on the land and receive proceeds from same during his life time.

Said land cannot be sold, ~~traded~~ mortgaged or given away.

At the death of Frank M. Willis complete control of said land goes to George Emerson Bassett who, under the same clause, is to have control and benefit of said property during his life time.

Title of the property herein described shall remain in the control of a direct descendant of Amous Herbert and Mary E. Bassett. Direct descendants now eligible are: Edna Bassett Haworth; Bill Haworth; Roy Bassett; Clark Bassett; Sam Bassett, Jr. and Frank N. MacKnight. A wife or husband of such descendant cannot control or have control of any ~~credit~~ interest in said property. Said wife or husband shall not control same for a minor child.

Should any devisee in control of said land fail to pay taxes on same the county treasurer of Moffat County, Colorado shall appoint an agent to pay such taxes by sale of produce from the land and notify the next of kin who is eligible, who may pay such taxes and take a life control of said property.

All improvements placed upon said land shall become the property of the land and cannot be removed.

The place shall be kept in good clean condition, ditches, fences, etc.

All the rest of my property shall become the property of Frank M. Willis.

Dated this 7 day of March 1952.

_____
Witness

_____
Witness

Ann Bassett Willis
Ann Bassett Willis

After Ann's heart attack, she wrote her will and had it witnessed and notarized.
Museum of Northwest Colorado

When Ann's ashes were sent to Frank Willis following cremation in Salt Lake City, he could not bring himself to scatter the ashes over "her beloved birthplace of Brown's Park." According to Grace McClure in her biography, *The Bassett Women*, Ann's cremated ashes included "yellowish" clumps among the fine ashes. Frank felt he could not honor Ann's wishes, as the ashes were not entirely ashes, as it was believed Ann was cremated with her diamond ring, which made clumps of the ashes.

Whether this was the reason or the bereaved husband just could not part with his wife's remains, Ann's clumped ashes remained in the trunk of Frank's car for several years. A few years after Ann's death, as Frank's health declined, Crawford McKnight took him in. When Frank moved out of McKnight's cabin in Brown's Park to live out his days at a lonely nursing home, he left behind a note nailed to the cabin wall.

To my friends and neighbors everywhere.

My wish is that when I die is to be buryed on the top of the hill N. W. of my cabin. I want a plain wooden coffin made by me or some of my friends. I do not want any undertaker to touch me or have anything to do with my body. Artificial work does not appeal to me.

Frank Willis.

Frank Willis moved into the Moffat Rest Home at Craig, where he could get proper care and medical attention. On Tuesday, July 16, 1963, Francis "Frank" Willis died at the age of 79. The *Empire Courier* printed the obituary in the July 25, 1963, issue:

Graveside Services Held Sunday For Frank Willis

Graveside services were held at the Brown's Park Cemetery Sunday at 2:00 p.m. for Francis (Frank) Willis, 79, with the Reverend Ella Beyer of the Maybell Congregational Church officiating.

Mr. Willis died Tuesday, July 16th, at the Moffat Rest Home in Craig after failing health of several years.

Surviving Mr. Willis is one daughter Sister Mary Elene Willis of St. Euphrasia School of Batesburg, South Carolina.

Josie and a few of the McKnight grandchildren attended Frank's funeral service. He was buried according to his wishes on a small hill not far from his cabin, but in the Brown's Park Cemetery.

Following the funeral, Josie and her grandchildren—all adults by this time, finally buried the remains of Ann Bassett Bernard Willis in the Bassett family cemetery. Fearing looting or vandalism, Josie did not want a marker for her sister's grave site. Ann was finally resting peacefully in her beloved Brown's Park. She once wrote, "Brown's Park is the only thing I ever selfishly loved."

Shortly before her death in 1956, Ann answered a reporter's question with this statement: "I've done everything they said I did and a helluva lot more."

The Bassett family cemetery where Josie Bassett eventually buried her sister Ann's ashes in an unmarked spot. *Museum of Northwest Colorado*

CHAPTER NOTES AND SOURCE INFORMATION

Francis "Frank" Willis spent the summer of 1917 with Hiram "Hi" Bernard, caring for cattle near the Green River, west of the Bassett ranch. Willis would later recount the events and recollections concerning Bernard in his unpublished manuscript, *Confidentially Told*.

Bernard's quotes are from *Confidentially Told*, the unpublished manuscript by Frank Willis.

Ann Bassett Willis' life experiences appeared in a four-part series published in the Colorado Historical Society's *Colorado Magazine*. The series, titled, "Queen Ann of Brown's Park," ran in Volume XXIX January 1952, Volume XXIX April 1952, Volume XXIX October 1952, Volume XXX January 1953. They are available at the Denver Public Library, as well as the Museum of Northwest Colorado, Craig, Colorado. Unless otherwise noted, the quotes attributed to Ann are from this work.

Court records involving Elbert "Eb" Bassett's fraud case are found in the Moffat County Court House. Copies are also in the archives of the Museum of Northwest Colorado, Craig, Colorado.

Many letters of Edna Bassett Haworth, the daughter of Ann's brother, George, can be found in the archives of the Museum of Northwest Colorado.

Edith McKnight Jensen's quote is from taped recordings in the Dejournette family files. Also see DeJournette, Dick and Daun, *One Hundred Years of Brown's Park and Diamond Mountain*, pg. 332.

Ann Bassett Willis writes of her experiences with the U. S. Forest Service in detail in "Queen Ann of Brown's Park," *Colorado Magazine*, January 1953.

Charles Kelly's *The Outlaw Trail: The Story of Butch Cassidy and the Wild Bunch*, originally published in 1938, was the book that so enraged both Ann and her sister, Josie. In his revised edition, published in 1959, by the Devin-Adair Company in New York, Kelly states he met Ann and that after a few interviews, she "warmed" to him. Ann never mentions such a meeting, but expresses disdain for the writer in her memoirs and several letters. In the last chapter of the revised edition, Kelly professes to give

Ann's side of the story, which does not in any way conform with historical fact, or Ann's accounts of the various events he recounts. The most outrageous account by Kelly is that after Matt Rash's murder, Ann retrieved cattle that she had supposedly sold to Rash but was never paid. On page 354 Kelly wrote: "Because of this, it was reported she and Rash were sweethearts and he had remembered her in his will." This is pure fabrication on Kelly's part. Not only would Ann never say such a thing, but it was common knowledge throughout the Park, not to mention the available newspapers, that the two were engaged to be married. Further, during the probate process, a will was never found, again further evidence of Kelly's many fabrications.

Ann Bassett Willis' letter to Esther Campbell can be found in the archives of the Vernal Public Library, Vernal, Utah. In this letter to Esther Campbell, Ann mentions the castration of J. S. Hoy. This had been a rumor floated throughout Brown's Park for years, even Hiram "Hi" Bernard mentioned it. In my conversations with his grandnephew, Valentine Hoy IV, he would neither confirm nor deny the rumor. However, the family history and genealogy of the J. S. Hoy family indicate the rumors were true. References include a possible medical procedure as well as a nefarious situation. It is also interesting to note that J. S. Hoy married twice, neither union producing children.

Rosalie Miles DeJournette's quotes are in the DeJournette family files. Also see DeJournette, Dick and Daun, *One Hundred Years of Brown's Park and Diamond Mountain*, pg. 225.

EPILOGUE

Every few years the subject of the mysterious Etta (Ethel) Place comes around to Ann Bassett of Brown's Park, Colorado. The supposition is based on Ann's presence in Brown's Park, one of the many hideouts for the Wild Bunch, as well as the many claims of romantic involvements with members of the outlaw gang. Curiously enough, in Ann's memoirs, where she is known to have exaggerated a few of her exploits, she never claimed to be romantically involved with any of the members of the Wild Bunch gang of outlaws, in particular, Harry Alonzo Longabaugh, alias, The Sundance Kid. With all her many exaggerations, she never claimed to be Etta Place, the known girlfriend/common-law wife of the Sundance Kid.

Nor could she, for she wasn't.

Nevertheless, over the years writers have espoused the ridiculous theory that Ann Bassett was indeed Etta Place. The history of Ann Bassett's life has been well documented in several publications regarding the history of Brown' Park and the integral part Ann played. From her birth in 1878, the first white child born in what was then known as Brown's Hole, to her vendetta against the cattle barons and subsequent triumphant acquittal of cattle theft charges, Ann's history can be found in court documents, newspaper coverage and in various first-hand accounts. There are also volumes of newspaper stories written about Ann, including her time at school, her engagement to Matt Rash, the murders of both Isom Dart and Matt Rash, and her legal fights in Routt County courtrooms.

Another outrageous allegation of the Etta Place/Ann Bassett connection hinges on the prostitution theory. Many historians have speculated that Etta Place may have been a prostitute. The most outlandish assertion of Ann Bassett being a prostitute, thereby furthering the Place/Bassett theory, is evidenced in the publication of *Red Light Women of the Rocky Mountains*, published in 2009 by the University of New Mexico Press. By the very title of the book, the author asserts that Ann Bassett was a prostitute, the first such assertion. On page 329, the author writes: "Although Ann Bassett was the daughter of a prominent rancher at Brown's Park (also known as Brown's Hole) along the Green River who was good friends with Butch, it is suspected she may have also have worked from time to time as a prostitute." The author gives a source footnote (#136, page 444), citing Richard Patterson's 1998 biography of Butch Cassidy, pages 98 and 178, as well as Pearl Baker's 1965 book, *The Wild Bunch at Robbers Roost*, page 173. After checking these two sources in detail, and the particular pages cited, neither author made such a claim.

An even more preposterous Etta Place/Ann Bassett connection was put forth in the 1992 self-published book, "Queen Ann Bassett: Alias Etta Place" by Doris Karren Burton. This author claims that Ann led a double life, dating Cassidy as Ann Bassett, and dating the Sundance Kid as Etta Place. Although this is undeniably false, not to mention absurd, as both outlaws

These two photographs of two very different women have often been compared with some believing they are the same person.

knew Ann from their time at the Bassett ranch, a fact the author apparently didn't consider or didn't research. Careful research would have led to Ann Bassett's obvious presence in Brown's Park in 1900, the year Burton writes of. Her engagement to Matt Rash was well known when Rash was murdered that summer by Tom Horn, whom Ann immediately suspected and personally alerted the Route County sheriff. Ann spends the next three months in probate court as the Rash estate is settled.

Burton offers up as her only proof, the only known photograph of Etta Place and the well-known photo of the beautiful young Ann Bassett. Placing the photos side by side she points out similar facial features of the two women, using Dr. Thomas G. Kyle of the Computer Research Group at Los Alamos National Laboratory, as her expert. Their final conclusion, declaring that there could be no doubt that the two women were one and the same was that both photographs feature evidence of a cowlick at the top of the forehead. The problem with this photographic analysis is that the photograph of Etta Place is a reversed image to match the angle of Ann Bassett's photo.

The author further indicates that when Ann Bassett is "absent from historical records," Etta Place is traveling with Butch and Sundance and when Etta is absent from historical records, Ann Bassett's whereabouts are accounted for. It's clear Burton did not take sufficient time to research the life of Ann Bassett.

Sadly, the inaccurate account put forth by Burton is repeated in other works. An example is *The Roadside History of Utah*, published by Mountain Press Publishing in 1999. Perusing the index, I found, "Bassett, Ann. See Place, Etta." The entry for Etta Place is found on pages 4 and 214. The author says that Etta Place and Butch Cassidy, "hid out in Brown's Park," with no mention of the Sundance Kid, on page 4. On page 214, the author writes: "It is possible that Ann Bassett of Brown's Park took the name of Etta Place," without any supporting evidence.

The following timeline chronicles the events and whereabouts of both women, and should prove, once and for all, that Etta (Ethel) Place and Anna M. Bassett were indeed, two very different women.

May 12, 1878–It is an undeniable fact that Anna M. Bassett was born to Herbert and Elizabeth Bassett in Brown's Hole, Colorado, a small ranching community at the northwest corner of the state, bordering with Utah to the west and Wyoming to the north. She is the third of five children to be raised in the area her mother will rename Brown's Park.

The woman later known as Ethel Place, may have been born in Texas in 1876, according to the Pinkerton archives. Years later, her given name is translated to "Etta," presumably by Pinkerton detectives, and first found in print in law enforcement reports and the media in 1906, following her sojourn with Butch Cassidy (Robert LeRoy Parker) and The Sundance Kid (Harry Longabough) to Buenos Aires, Argentina.

1893 to 1895–Ann attends St. Mary's of the Wasatch Academy in Salt Lake City, Utah, and later an Eastern school. In her memoirs, she says the experience left "a deep impression." Ann hosts the 1896 Thanksgiving dinner for all the families in Brown's Park. From her memoirs, Ann says guests included Matt Rash, Isom Dart, Elza Lay, and Harry Roudenbaugh. If this is the Sundance Kid, she obviously didn't know him very well, as she misspells his surname.

Several writers have asserted that Ethel "Etta" Place was either a prostitute or a school teacher, having attended Miss Porter's School for Girls in Boston, Massachusetts. "Miss Porter's" is an error found in Grace McClure's *The Bassett Women*, where she refers to the school in Boston. Miss Porter's School for Girls is located in Connecticut. It is interesting to note that during further research, it was learned that the Porter School for Girls, in Connecticut, has received numerous calls from researchers. Ann Bassett never attended this institution, nor are there any records regarding Ethel "Etta" Place. In Ann Bassett's own words, she claimed she attended Mrs. Potter's School for Girls, in Boston, Massachusetts, which is also correctly stated in John Rolfe Burroughs' account of Brown's Park history, *Where the Old West Stayed Young*.

This is an example of an error repeated by various writers as fact without further research. In this case, it becomes one of the many twisted tales that writers have pointed to claiming the women are one and the same.

Added into this mix of Porter and Potter confusion is the Fanny Porter bordello in San Antonio, Texas, where Butch and Sundance were both known to frequent. Some writers have speculated that this was Ethel "Etta" Place's place of employment and possibly where she met the Sundance Kid, once again giving rise to the prostitution theory. Or it could have been Madam Mary Porter's bordello in Fort Worth, Texas, where the two met. The speculation will no doubt continue.

However, Anna M. Bassett was never in Texas during this time.

1896–Ann facilitates several romantic meetings for her friend Elza Lay, and Maud Davis of Ashley Valley, Utah. With Ann's help, a local minister is spirited to a quiet meadow location along the Green River to marry the two. Maud, a friend of Ann's and who also knew Etta Place, would later say that Etta was "the most beautiful woman she had ever known."

During the winter of 1896-97, Elza and Maud Lay are at Robber's Roost in Utah with Butch Cassidy, the Sundance Kid, and Etta Place. The group remains there until the Castle Gate Payroll Robbery, committed by Cassidy and Lay, on April 21, 1897.

January 9, 1897–The *Craig Courier* reports a Christmas dinner event hosted by the J.W. Lowell, Jr. family of Lily Park, Colorado. In attendance are the James McKnight family (Ann's sister, Josie), Sam and Elbert Bassett (Ann's brothers), M. M. Rash, and Miss Ann Bassett.

Etta Place is at the Robber's Roost hideout near Hanksville, Utah, leaving sometime after April 21, 1897.

July 8, 1900–Matt Rash is found dead in his cabin on Cold Spring Mountain. He had been shot three times from the cabin doorway. Ann is devastated and enraged at the murder of her fiancé. Three days later, Ann confronts deputy sheriff Charley Sparks, explaining her belief that the stranger Thomas Hicks, alias Tom Horn, is the murderer.

August 1, 1900–Ann Bassett is in the county seat of Routt County, Steamboat Springs, filing a probate petition regarding the estate of Maddison Matt Rash.

Many historians believe Etta Place is in Texas, working as either a teacher or a prostitute at Fanny Porter's bordello in San Antonio, a place frequented by members of the Wild Bunch outlaw gang, including the Sundance Kid.

These signatures demonstrates the obvious difference in handwriting styles of Etta Place and Ann Bassett. *Ethel Place signature is courtesy of Donna Ernst*

October 3, 1900–Isom Dart, Bassett ranch hand and family friend, is shot to death by a single bullet to the head. Among the witnesses are George and Sam Bassett, Ann's brothers. The entire Bassett family is devastated at yet another murder.

October 12, 1900–Routt County Probate Court Judge Isaac Voice, closes the Matthew Rash estate, with Ann traveling to Steamboat Springs to receive a monetary settlement.

The whereabouts of Etta Place at this time are unknown.

November 1900–Ann is on a self-imposed vendetta against the large cattle ranchers in general, and Ora Haley in particular. She would protect, defend, and defy those who attempted to overtake her beloved Brown's Park. Ann roams the area daily, on horseback with her rifle, turning back Haley's Two Bar cattle at times by actions that are questioned by law enforcement. "No other stockmen were responsible for what I did. I had no support but a Winchester rifle and plenty of ammunition. The herds did not go west of the divide but were turned out east of Brown's Park."

November 1900, the Sundance Kid reunites with Etta Place in Fort Worth, Texas. On Wednesday, November 21, 1900, Sundance poses with members of the Wild Bunch, including Butch Cassidy, Will Carver, Ben Kilpatrick, and Harvey (Kid Curry) Logan, for a photograph at the Swartz View portrait studio. It becomes known as the "Fort Worth Five" photo, identifying the members of the Wild Bunch for the first time. When law enforcement obtains a copy of the photo, the outlaws split up. Cassidy and Sundance agree to meet in New York City, where they will sail for Argentina.

January 1901–Ann spends time in Vernal, Utah, visiting with family and friends before leaving by stage to Denver, where she will board a train for Texas.

Sundance and Etta Place leave Texas, travel together as "Mr. and

Mrs. Harry A. Place," arriving in Pennsylvania in January 1901, for a visit with the Longabaugh family.

February 1901– Traveling under the name, "Mr. and Mrs. Harry A. Place" the Sundance Kid and Etta Place each sign the register at Mrs. Catherine Taylor's boarding house in New York City. Two days later, the couple pose for the infamous photo that will eventually be seen on wanted posters around the world. It will be the first known image of the elusive Etta Place.

The Vernal Express reports: "Miss Ann Bassett left on this morning's stage for Texas. She will visit at Grand Junction and Denver enroute."

It should be quite obvious by these dates that Ann Bassett could not be at two different places halfway across the country at the same time.

On February 9, 1901, the *Craig Courier* reports that Ann Bassett is taken to the hospital in Grand Junction, Colorado, with pneumonia. Her trip to Texas is delayed.

On February 20, 1901, Etta, along with Sundance and Butch Cassidy, sail from New York City on the Herminius, for Buenos Aires, Argentina.

1902–Ann Bassett is in the saddle day after day. She and a friend "...would spot a little bunch of Two Bar cattle down by the river. We forced them into the water. Those that made it to the other side, wandered off into the badlands. In any event, they were lost to the Two Bar, who didn't round up west of the Green. We were especially active during 1902 and 1903, and we cost Ora Haley hundreds of cattle."

Etta Place remains in Cholila, Argentina with Sundance and Butch until a brief visit to America in the spring of 1902, where she and the Sundance Kid are identified by the Pinkertons from an unidentified hospital report dated May 10, 1902, in Atlantic City, New Jersey. The couple sail for Buenos Aires on July 10, 1902.

1904–Creating a division in the Two Bar outfit, Ann courts and eventually marries the manager of the Two Bar, Hi Bernard, on April 13, 1904. The couple settled into married life and expanded their cattle herd. Ora Haley fights back, firing his manager and eventually taking Ann to court for cattle rustling not once, but twice.

* Etta Place and the Sundance Kid return to America. A Pinkerton memo dated October 24, 1904, states that the couple is in the Fort Worth, Texas area.

1905–Ann and Hi Bernard form The Bassett-Bernard Cattle Company, located on Douglas Mountain in Brown's Park. Bernard also secures the water rights in the area.

Two Buenos Aires newspapers, the *La Nacion* and the *La Prensa*, both dated December 24, 1905, report the robbery of the Banco de la Nacion in Villa Mercedes, Argentina. Both papers identify Butch Cassidy, the Sundance Kid, and Ethel "Etta" Place as the perpetrators of the bank robbery.

1907–Ann and Hi Bernard continued to increase The Bassett-Bernard Cattle Company, encompassing some twelve hundred acres where they wintered their joint herds of cattle. Bernard recounts a harrowing trip he and Ann take across the Green River in January, 1907.

A Pinkerton memo dated January 15, 1907, states that Ethel "Etta" Place and the Sundance Kid were living near Norquin, Province of Neuquen, Argentina. However, renowned researchers, Dan Buck and Ann Meadows have evidence that the couple were in Chile. Either way, the two locations were half a world away from Ann Bassett Bernard's home on Douglas Mountain where she was busy raising cattle.

At this point Etta Place disappears from the historical record. Some writers place her in Denver at various dates for various reasons such as an "emergency" appendectomy, which for some unfathomable reason could not be performed in Argentina or Chile. Another reason offered by writers is that she returned to America because she was pregnant, also unrealistic.

The historical record from this point for Ann Bassett is quite available for anyone wishing to do the research. Her vendetta against Ora Haley is well documented throughout the years of the known sightings of Ethel "Etta" Place, and continues through two court fights concerning cattle theft in 1911 and again in 1913. Acquitted of all charges, Ann Bassett goes on to live a long life, dying in 1956 at the age of seventy-eight.

BIBLIOGRAPHY

Primary Sources

Bassett, Ann. Unpublished diary. Uintah County Library.

Bassett, Ann. Unpublished memoirs. Denver Public Library.

Bassett, Ann. Unpublished manuscript, *History of Brown's Park*. Uintah County Library.

Bassett, Josephine. Taped interviews by Murl Messersmith, July 6, 1961. Dinosaur National Monument archives, Jensen, Utah. Type-written transcript available at the Museum of Northwest Colorado, Craig, Colorado.

Campbell. Esther. Notes and correspondence. Dinosaur National Monument archives.

Campbell. Esther. Letters and correspondence. Uintah County Library.

Hoy, J.S. *History of Brown's Hole*. Courtesy of Valentine Hoy, IV.

Hoy, J.S., Manuscript. Colorado History Center.

Moffat County Court records, Craig, Colorado.

Tennent, William. Personal remembrances and notes. Museum of Northwest Colorado.

Willis, Ann Bassett. Letters, notes and personal items. Museum of Northwest Colorado.

Willis, Ann Bassett. *Scars and Two Bars*. *Moffat County Mirror* series published in April 1943. Partial memoir archived at the Museum of Northwest Colorado.

Willis, Ann Bassett. "Queen Ann of Brown's Park." *Colorado Magazine*, Volume XXIX, April 1952, Volume XXIX, January 1952, Volume XXIX, October 1952, Volume XXX, January 1953. Denver Public Library.

Willis, Frank. Unpublished manuscript, *Confidentially Told*. Museum of Northwest Colorado.

Interviews and Correspondence

Buck, Dan, Western Historian. July 28, 29, 2016. August 1, 2, 3, 2016.

Davidson, Dan, Director, Museum of Northwest Colorado. September 20, 2009. March 18, 2011. July 25, 26, 2014, January 26, 29, 2015. June 1, 2, 3, 2015. February 8, 9, 2016.

Davies, Kathie, Bureau of Land Management, Vernal, Utah. August 1, 2, 3, 2016.

Denzer, Lee Ann, Uintah County Museum and Regional History Center. August 1, 2, 3, 2016.

Fuller, Michelle, Uintah County Library and Regional History Center. August 1–8, 2016.

Gerber, Jan, Museum of Northwest Colorado. September 12, 20, 21, 22, 2008. June 11, 2009. April 8, 2012. January 25, 2015. June 1, 2, 3, 5, 29, 2015.

Hoy, Valentine IV. July 25, 26, 2014.

Newspapers

The various local newspaper archives accessed for this work are noted in the exact quotes used throughout the text. They include:

The Colorado Pantograph
The Craig Courier
The Craig Empire
The Denver Post
The Empire Courier
The Moffat County Mirror
The Rock Springs Miner
The Rock Springs Rocket
The Steamboat Pilot
The Vernal Express

Archives and Additional Sources

American Heritage Center. University of Wyoming at Laramie.
Colorado County and Federal Census records.
Dinosaur National Monument.
Museum of Northwest Colorado.
National Bureau of Land Management.
Tread of Pioneers Museum. Steamboat Springs, Colorado.
Utah Department of Community and Culture.
Uintah County Library. Vernal, Utah.
Uintah County Heritage Museum. Vernal, Utah.
Utah State Historical Society Research Center and Collections.
Records of Private Amos Herbert Bassett. United States National Archives. Copies in the archives of Museum of Northwest Colorado.

Books

Athearn, Frederic J. *An Isolated Empire: A History of Northwestern Colorado*.
Ball, Larry D. *Tom Horn; In Life and Legend*. University of Oklahoma Press, 2014.
Burroughs, John Rolfe. *Where the Old West Stayed Young*. William Morrow and Company, 1962.
Carlson, Chip. *Tom Horn: Blood on the Moon*. High Plains Press, 2001.
DeJournette, Dick and Daun. *One Hundred Years of Brown's Park and Diamond Mountain*. DeJournette Enterprises, 1996.
Ellison, Douglas W. *David Lant: The Vanished Outlaw*. Midstates Printing, Inc., 1988.
Ernst, Donna. *The Sundance Kid: The Life of Harry Alonzo Longabaugh*. University of Oklahoma, 2009.
Gulick, Bill. *Man Hunt: The Pursuit of Harry Tracy*. Caxton Press, 1999.
Horn, Tom. *Life of Tom Horn, Written By Himself*. University of Oklahoma Press, 1964.

Hughel, Avvon Chew. *The Chew Bunch in Brown's Park*. Scrimshaw Press, 1970.

Kouris, Diana Allen. *The Romantic and Notorious History of Brown's Park*. Wolverine Gallery Publishers, 1988.

McClure, Grace. *The Bassett Women*. Swallow Press, 1985.

Patterson, Richard. *Butch Cassidy: A Biography*. University of Nebraska Press, 1998.

Warner, Matt. *Last of the Bandit Riders...Revisited*. Big Moon Traders, 2000.

Wommack, Linda. *From the Grave: A Roadside Guide to Colorado's Pioneer Cemeteries*. Caxton Press, 1998.

Journals and Magazines

(Author Unknown). "Profile of Josephine Bassett." *Life Magazine*, April, 1948.

Monaghan, Jay. Moffat County CWA Papers, Colorado History Center.

Wommack, Linda. "The Ann Bassett/Etta Place Timeline." *Wild West History Journal*, April, 2012.

Wommack, Linda. "Ann Bassett of Colorado." *The Colorado Countrylife Magazine*, April, 1998.

INDEX

A

Ayer, Charles E., "Charlie" 109, 114, 120, 130, 131, 132, 134, 139

B

Bassett, Amos Herbert 16, 17, 18, 26, 28, 33, 92, 199

Bassett, Elbert "Eb" 36, 51, 52, 60, 85, 88, 93, 97, 103, 110, 123, 130, 136, 137, 145, 146, 154 156, 158, 161, 178, 181, 190, 199, 201, 202, 203, 204, 205, 207, 209, 224, 231

Bassett, George 36, 50, 51, 59, 85, 127, 128, 130, 137, 154, 156, 158, 161, 199, 202, 203, 208, 211, 224, 233

Bassett, Josephine "Josie" 7, 18, 26, 27, 28, 31, 32, 33, 34, 36, 37, 38, 39, 42, 52, 53, 54, 57, 58, 61, 62, 65, 67, 68, 69, 70, 71, 72, 73, 74, 76, 78, 83, 88, 89, 90, 91, 97, 100, 101, 103, 116, 117, 123, 126, 127, 129, 135, 145, 146, 155, 156, 160, 170, 176, 191, 193, 196, 197, 199, 201, 202, 203, 207, 213, 214, 215, 216, 217, 220, 223, 224, 231

Bassett, Mary Elizabeth Chamberlain Miller 17, 18, 61, 62, 64, 65

Bassett Ranch 7, 11, 30, 39, 46, 47, 48, 49, 56, 57, 58, 61, 67, 70, 71, 80, 81, 82, 85, 86, 88, 89, 91, 92, 93, 98, 99, 100, 102, 113, 116, 121, 125 130, 135, 137, 139, 145, 152, 159, 170, 190, 192, 197, 199, 204, 210, 220, 224, 229, 233

Bassett, Samuel Clark II 13, 14, 16

Bassett, Samuel "Sam" 16, 18, 19, 20, 21, 26, 27, 31, 32, 33, 36, 38, 60, 61, 76, 78, 103, 115, 116, 127, 128, 135, 141, 156, 199, 214, 219, 231, 233

Bennett, John Jack "Judge" 7, 82, 83, 84, 85, 89, 90, 91, 93, 96, 216

Bernard, Hiram "Hi" 8, 67, 100, 102, 105, 106, 107, 108, 109, 110, 111, 117, 119, 120, 129, 132, 133, 134, 135, 138, 139, 143, 148, 149, 150, 151, 153, 154, 155, 156, 157, 158, 159, 160, 161, 162, 163, 169, 170, 171, 173, 174, 175, 176, 179, 180, 181, 185, 190, 192, 193, 195, 196, 197, 198, 201, 220, 224, 225, 235

Bowen, Chick 179, 181, 182, 183, 184, 187, 191

Brown, Baptiste 12

Brown's Hole (See Brown's Park)

Brown's Park 1, 3, 4, 5, 7, 8, 10, 11, 12, 19, 21, 26, 28, 31, 32, 37, 38, 39, 42, 43, 44, 45, 47, 48, 52, 55, 58, 59, 60, 61, 62, 65, 67, 68, 69, 71, 72, 73, 74, 75, 76, 77, 79, 80, 81, 82, 83, 84, 85, 91, 92, 95, 96, 100, 103, 104, 105, 107, 108, 109, 111, 112, 114, 116, 117, 119, 120, 122, 124, 125, 126, 127, 129, 130, 131, 132, 134, 135, 137, 138, 139, 140, 141, 142, 143, 145, 146, 149, 150, 151, 154, 155, 157, 164, 169, 170, 173, 174, 175, 182, 187, 190, 191, 193, 197, 199, 200, 201, 202, 203, 205, 207, 209, 210, 211, 212, 213, 214, 216, 219, 220, 222, 223, 224, 225, 227, 228, 229, 230, 233, 235

C

Campbell, Esther Anderson 5, 8, 35, 52, 72, 78, 101, 158, 170, 176, 191, 213, 214, 216, 217, 220, 225

Carson, Christopher "Kit" 13,14

Chew, Leath Avvon 8, 144, 145, 146, 147, 148, 161, 170

Coble, John 109, 110,133,148

Crouse, Charles "Charlie" 25, 34, 40, 41, 66, 67, 68, 79, 83, 100, 114, 115, 124, 130, 156, 212

Cassidy, "Butch" (See Parker, George Leroy)

Conway, Asbury B. 21, 22, 24, 25, 32, 33, 40

Curry, George "Flat Nose" 69

D

Dart, Isom 47, 49, 51, 59, 60, 77, 93, 105, 115, 117, 123, 126, 127, 128, 129, 130, 137, 138, 140, 142, 149, 182, 211, 227, 230, 233

Davenport, Joseph 38, 78, 93, 94, 95, 110, 112, 113, 115, 119, 132, 140, 141, 145

Davenport, Thomas 25, 34, 35, 38, 58, 60, 93, 112

Davidson, Carl 49, 104, 114, 130, 135

Davis, Matilda Maud 81, 82, 231

Demsher, John 128

E

Edwards, Mattie 209

F

Farnham, Ethan Allen 85, 87, 89, 91, 92, 93, 94, 95, 98, 111

Fitch, Jack 47, 59, 60

Fort Davy Crockett 13, 15

G

Gooding, A.M. 174, 175, 177, 185,186

Gunn, Jack 45

H

Haley, Ora 7, 8, 53, 80, 104, 106, 107, 108, 109, 110, 111, 119, 132, 133, 134, 135, 137, 138, 139, 141, 142, 143, 144, 145, 148, 150, 151, 153, 154, 155, 157, 164, 165, 166, 167, 169, 170, 171, 173, 174, 175, 178, 179, 180, 181, 182, 183, 185, 186, 187, 188, 189, 199, 209, 233, 234, 235, 236

Herrera, Juan José "Mexican Joe" 20, 21, 22, 23, 24, 25, 27, 41, 53

Herrera, Pablo 20

Hicks, Thomas (James) 110, 116, 117, 118, 121, 123, 127, 128, 129, 130, 135, 138, 148, 232

Hindle, Henry "Harry" 25, 57, 91, 128, 138

Horn, Tom (see Thomas Hicks)

Hoy, Adea A. 41, 42, 43, 45, 59, 165
Hoy, Benjamin Frank 41, 42, 43, 45, 165
Hoy, Henry "Harry" 38, 41, 42, 43, 45, 59, 65, 165
Hoy, James Jessie Smith 4, 7, 8, 12, 19, 20, 22, 23, 24, 25, 28, 41, 42, 43, 44, 45, 48, 53, 62, 65, 79, 82, 84, 85, 90, 92, 95, 97, 98, 101, 128, 131, 135, 145, 156, 159, 165, 171, 179, 186, 188, 191, 193, 195, 196, 198, 215, 225
Hoy, Valentine Shade 4, 7, 23, 24, 28, 40, 41, 42, 43, 45, 53, 60, 83, 85, 86, 87, 88, 92, 93, 95, 96, 98, 101, 165, 170, 195, 196, 214, 225

J

Jaynes, Henry 38
Jaynes, Jennie 38, 56
Johnson, Patrick Louis "P. L." 82, 83, 85, 94, 95, 96, 98, 99
Jones, Joe 125, 126, 190

K

Kinney, Tim 103, 110

L

Lant, David 7, 84, 85, 86, 87, 92, 94, 95, 97, 98, 99, 170
Lay, William Ellsworth "Elza" 7, 69, 70, 76, 77, 79, 81, 101, 104, 204, 206, 230, 231
Logan, Harvey "Kid Curry" 79, 233
Longabough, Harry "The Sundance Kid" 69, 79, 71, 101, 227, 228, 229, 230, 231, 232, 233, 234, 235
Lyons, Lilton 91

M

McCarty, Tom 69, 70, 79
McDougall, Angus 47, 59, 60
McKnight, Crawford 72, 91, 197, 202, 217, 222
McKnight, Edith 201, 204, 206, 224
McKnight, Herbert "Chick" 92, 160, 201, 204, 206
McKnight, James "Jim" 47, 51, 58, 61, 72, 83, 86, 87, 88, 89, 90, 91, 92, 93, 95, 96, 97, 98, 103, 116, 120, 123, 126, 128, 129, 133, 145, 156, 231
Meek, Joseph 14
Meeker Massacre 34, 52
Meldrum, Robert "Bob" 182, 183, 184, 186, 187, 191
Meyers, Felix 95, 121
Miles, Rosalie 47, 146, 149, 157, 170, 219, 225

N

Neiman, Charles Willis 83, 84, 85, 86, 87, 88, 92, 93, 95, 96, 97, 98, 99, 124, 125

ABOUT THE AUTHOR

A Colorado native, Linda Wommack, is a Colorado historian and historical consultant. She has written eight books on Colorado history, including *Murder in the Mile High City, Colorado's Landmark Hotels, From the Grave: Colorado's Pioneer Cemeteries, Our Ladies of the Tenderloin: Colorado's Legends in Lace, Colorado History for Kids,* and *Colorado's Historic Mansions and Castles.* She has also contributed to two anthologies concerning Western Americana.

Linda has been a contributing editor for *True West Magazine* since 1995. She has been a staff writer for *Wild West Magazine,* contributing a monthly article since 2004. She has written for the *Tombstone Epitaph* since 1993, the nation's oldest continuously published newspaper,. Linda also writes for several publications throughout her state.

Linda's research has been used in several documentary accounts for the national Wild West History Association, historical treatises of the Sand Creek Massacre, as well as critical historic aspects for the new Lawman & Outlaw Museum in Cripple Creek, Colorado, which opened in 2007.

Linda feeds her passion for history with activities in many local, state, and national preservation projects. She participates in historical venues that include speaking engagements and hosting tours, and is involved in historical reenactments across the state.

As a longtime member of the national Western Writers of America, she has served as a judge for the acclaimed national Spur Awards in Western Americana literature for eight years. She is a member of both the State and National Cemetery Preservation Associations, the Gilpin County Historical Society, the national Wild West History Association, and an honorary lifetime member of the Pikes Peak Heritage Society. As a member of Women Writing the West, for the past seven years Linda has organized quarterly meetings for the Colorado members of WWW, served on the 2014 WWW Convention Steering Committee, and currently serves as a board member.

≈ ANN BASSETT ≈

◇◇◇◇◇◇◇

Colorado's 👑 *Cattle* Queen

This is the first full-length biography of an extraordinary woman in Colorado's history.

Anna Marie Bassett was the first white child born in the notorious outlaw region of Colorado known as Brown's Park. She knew outlaws such as Butch Cassidy and the Sundance Kid and became lifelong friends with Elza Lay.

When Tom Horn, hired by Ora Haley, owner of the Two Bar Cattle enterprise, murdered her fiancé Matt Rash, Ann Bassett launched a personal vendetta against Haley and the Two Bar ranch.

"Throwing caution to the winds, I pushed cattle off the range. I had to work alone. My neighbors did not support me in this, my challenge to Haley, and defiance of law and order. No other stockmen were responsible for what I did. I turned the heat against myself by an open declaration of war."

This is the account of Colorado's Cattle Queen, Ann Bassett, told largely in her own words and supported by friends and enemies alike.

"Ann was a visionary and up in the air a good part of the time."
– Josephine Bassett Morris

"We came into Brown's Park to run the nesters out. We started it, but Elizabeth Bassett [Ann's mother] finished it, and she finished it good!"
– J. S. Hoy

"I'll never forget seeing this beautiful woman riding her horse as if molded to the saddle. Thick, reddish-brown hair peeked out from under a large white scarf tied beneath her chin. Her skin was flawless with shining eyes which flashed with fire and life. Every nine year-old has an idol; this lovely lady of twenty-seven years became mine immediately."
– Rosalie Miles DeJournette

"It was Ann's custom to collect these Two Bar animals and drive them into the Green River, using any help she could get, but generally the young folks with whom she was always a favorite. When crowded into the river, many of the cattle were swept into the canyon by the swift currents, and those that made the west and south bank drifted up Hoy Canyon to Wild Mountain and Diamond Mountain. Without any supervision, they soon fell into the hands of the riders, who used the 'long rope.'"
– Leath Avvon Chew

"Ann is not so much interested in seeing any human being as she is in rambling over the old Bassett Ranch and caressing every ugly, scaggy cedar in Brown's Park. She is blended into the rugged mountains around here and belongs to them."
– Hiram "Hi" Bernard

"Brown's Park brought back a poignant yearning to dash away and drive an avalanche of Two Bar cattle back across the divide. Then I would awaken from my dream to discover that I had been peeping into the past that cannot return. Live Two Bar cattle are conspicuously absent. The winds have buried all the dead ones."
– Ann Bassett

These people and Ann herself together provide the extraordinary story of Anna M. Bassett, Colorado's Cattle Queen.

"Brown's Park and its hills and valleys, is the only thing I ever selfishly loved."
– Ann Bassett